3

WITHDRAWN

MARKETS AND MORALS

MARKETS AND MORALS

Edited by

Gerald Dworkin

Department of Philosophy
University of Illinois—Chicago Circle

Gordon Bermant

Federal Judicial Center

Peter G. Brown

Center for Philosophy and Public Policy
University of Maryland

HEMISPHERE
PUBLISHING CORPORATION

Washington   London

A HALSTED PRESS BOOK

JOHN WILEY & SONS

New York   London   Sydney   Toronto

Hemisphere Publishing Corporation
1025 Vermont Ave., N.W., Washington, D.C. 20005

Distributed solely by Halsted Press, a Division of John Wiley & Sons, Inc., New York

1 2 3 4 5 6 7 8 9 0   D O D O   7 8 3 2 1 0 9 8 7

Library of Congress Cataloging in Publication Data

Main entry under title:

Markets and morals.

  Includes many of the papers presented at a three-day conference beginning May 9, 1974, at the Seattle Research Center of the Battelle Memorial Institute.
  Includes index.
  1. Economics—Congresses.   2. Capitalism—Congresses.   3. Property—Congresses.   I. Dworkin, Gerald, 1937–   II. Bermant, Gordon.
III. Brown, Peter, 1940–
HB72.M247   330   77-5904
ISBN 0-470-99169-0

Printed in the United States of America

CONTENTS

PREFACE

On May 9, 1974, thirty scholars gathered at the Seattle Research Center of the Battelle Memorial Institute for a three-day conference entitled "Markets and Morals." This volume includes many of the papers presented at the conference as well as one submitted subsequently.

The conference grew from conversations among the editors during the autumn of 1973. Our intent was to clarify issues at the intersection of economic theory and moral philosophy, in particular to investigate the foundations for claims that certain means of resource distribution and market control are morally preferable to others. This is an extraordinarily difficult task, for, among other problems, one runs head on into the need to make general assumptions about human nature that contemporary behavioral science can neither support nor reject. At this stage of our understanding, therefore, satisfactory intellectual closure is not to be had without the purchase of large psychological assumptions. Empirical support for the assumptions is so weak that they become, in fact, ideological, i.e., articles of faith or desire about human economic behavior.

Support for the conference and publication was provided by the Behavioral and Social Science Program of the Battelle Institute. The editors are very grateful to the officers of Battelle who were instrumental in the support of our efforts: T. W. Ambrose, E. R. Irish, and R. S. Paul deserve our special thanks. Ellen

Brandt, Barbara Hawley, and Julia Schairer of the Battelle Seattle Research Center Staff were very helpful at the time of the conference and thereafter. Finally, we are grateful to Faith Fogarty of Battelle for managing the manuscript through to a successful conclusion.

Gerald Dworkin
Gordon Bermant
Peter G. Brown

ABOUT THE EDITORS

Gerald Dworkin is professor of philosophy at the University of Illinois, Chicago Circle. He received his Ph.D. at the University of California, Berkeley, and has taught at Harvard, MIT, and the University of Washington. His main interests are in moral, political, and legal philosophy. He has published articles in philosophical and legal journals, and his most recent book (with N. J. Block) is *The IQ Controversy* (Pantheon Press).

Gordon Bermant is project director and research psychologist at the Federal Judicial Center, Washington, D.C. He was for seven years associated with the Battelle Memorial Institute, as research scientist in the Law and Justice Study Center, center fellow in the Battelle Seminar and Study Program, and coordinator of the Battelle Institute Program in the Behavioral and Social Sciences. He received the Ph.D. in psychology from Harvard University. He has been research fellow at the University of California, Berkeley, associate professor of psychology at the University of California, Davis, and affiliate professor of psychology at the University of Washington. He is coauthor of *Biological Bases of Sexual Behavior*, editor of *Perspectives on Animal Behavior,* and coeditor of *Primate Utilization and Conservation, The Ethics of Social Intervention* (forthcoming), and *Psychology and the Law.*

Peter G. Brown is director of the Center for Philosophy and Public Policy at the University of Maryland. He received his Ph.D. in political philosophy from Columbia University, and has taught at St. John's College, the University of Washington, and the University of Maryland. He has worked for the Urban Institute, Battelle, and the Academy for Contemporary Problems. As well as being author of numerous monographs and articles in legal and other periodicals, he is coeditor of *Food Policy: U.S. Responsibility in the Life and Death Choices*, forthcoming from the Free Press.

MARKETS AND MORALS

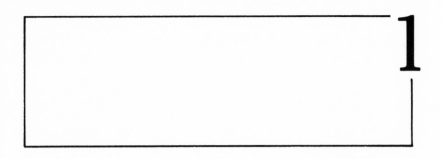

AN INTRODUCTION TO
MARKETS AND MORALS

GORDON BERMANT
Battelle Seattle Research Center

PETER G. BROWN
Center for Philosophy and Public Policy
University of Maryland

GERALD DWORKIN
Department of Philosophy
University of Illinois–Chicago Circle

Much current political debate centers on the appropriate criteria that should govern the production and consumption of various goods. In the area of educational financing, for example, we find arguments for and against the use of educational vouchers that would enable parents to send their children to schools of their choice. In the area of national defense, controversy exists concerning the merits of a draft versus those of a volunteer army. The recent attention paid to environmental issues leads to discussions of the best way to determine the

1

"acceptable" amount of pollution and the proper mechanisms for achieving that goal. With respect to energy policy, the debate concerns the appropriate methods of decreasing demand for gasoline: Shall we use the market device of raising prices or the command device of rationing? One of the major issues currently before the Congress concerns the question of how medical care ought to be financed and distributed.

In addition to these general themes, there are more particular issues that create intellectual and political controversy. Should people be allowed to buy drugs or sex? Should blood or organs of the body be saleable? Should income redistribution be in the form of cash or in-kind assistance? Should people be guaranteed a minimum income independently of their willingness to engage in productive labor?

Underlying these particular controversies are more abstract and theoretical assumptions about the proper approach to analyzing these issues and the best way to reason about the normative questions involved. In addition to policy debates, there are theoretical controversies among philosophers, economists, legal theorists, and behavioral scientists about the proper role of market mechanisms, either as guides to making correct policy decisions or as means to implementing such decisions.

The use of market theory as a guide to policy making is less familiar than the actual use of markets to distribute scarce resources. But in recent years legal theorists interested in determining rules of liability (say, for accidents) have used the theoretical apparatus developed by economists to provide answers to this problem (Calabresi, 1970; Coase, 1960). Using the model of a perfectly competitive market and the single normative premise of efficiency of resource allocation (defined as a state of affairs when nobody can be made better off, in his own estimation, without somebody else being made worse off), these theorists argue that liability rules should be formalized so that the distribution of costs best approximates the distribution that would be reached by bargaining in a perfectly competitive market (assuming there are no costs connected with bargaining). Similarly, public finance theorists have attempted to judge the value of goods financed by the public sector in terms of their estimates of the willingness of individuals to pay for the goods in a private market (Musgrave, 1959).

It is clear that various arguments for and against the use of markets rely on moral, political, psychological, and metaphysical assumptions. These assumptions are the boundaries within which we organize and relate our ideas about the efficiency and morality of commercial life. They impose structure, hence limits, on our economic thought. Yet they often pass unnoticed or unquestioned in the complex debates of economic policies and practices. We, therefore, invited a group of philosophers and economists to a conference at the Battelle Seattle Research Center, May 9-11, 1974. We asked them to address themselves in an explicit fashion to these assumptions and their supporting arguments. Taken together, the essays should provide the reader with new opportunities to understand and evaluate the usually implicit background of arguments about the worth and morality of particular economic practices.

As an organizational device, we asked the contributors to this volume to respond to the following general themes: (1) a historical view of the connections between the rise of market institutions and the ways in which individuals and societies perceive and conceptualize the world (both natural and social); (2) normative issues concerning markets (e.g., why we are justified in believing that some things ought to be for sale and others not; whether there ought to be markets for votes or sex or blood or food or human labor); (3) a discussion of these issues with respect to the distribution of health care.

HISTORICAL PERSPECTIVE

The Concept of the Market

Bernard Barber, a sociologist from Columbia University, discusses the historical development of the notion of the market in social theory. He argues that the notion of the market is so much a part of the economist's world view that little attention is paid to it as just one of the ways in which individuals can enter into exchange relationships with one another. Like the fish who ignores the water that surrounds it, the economist does not isolate the market for specific study.

Barber also calls attention to the functional prerequisites for differing forms of exchange—the presence of norms and institutions that provide the framework in which various exchange relations can take place. Thus, a system of market exchange is dependent on certain rules of property, a legal system that enforces those rules, certain conceptions of equity and efficiency, an educated population, the possibility of social mobility, and so forth.

Ideology and the Market

Walter Weisskopf, an economist from Roosevelt University, traces the development of various attempts to provide an ideological justification for the market system. Initially, the sanctification of the market was religious in nature. Economic success was interpreted as a sign of grace. Later, Social Darwinism justified competitive market behavior as a device for filtering out the unfit. Other justifications included the "invisible hand" theories and various arguments concerning the value of liberty, as manifested in voluntary exchanges.

Weisskopf argues that contemporary justifications have abandoned any appeal to the common good or public interest and rely on claims concerning the market as an efficient satisfier of individual, subjective preferences. And individual preferences are, from the point of view of economic analysis, simply a given—subject neither to evaluation nor to criticism. Weisskopf calls for a return to a more substantive value position that will provide ideals and guidelines to regulate the market.

In the discussion that followed these papers, a good deal of attention was paid to sorting out the essential features of a market system. Is the notion of an economizing, maximizing individual essential to a market, as opposed, say, to the kind of individual who prefers some kind of reciprocal (or gift-giving) system of exchange? Is exchange a sterile or productive form of action? What is the relationship between market exchange and zero-sum games?

Some topics that might lead to fruitful investigation include the connections (psychological or otherwise) between the emergence of individualism as an ideology and the rise of a market economy; various conceptions of freedom, duress, and equal bargaining power in a market economy; and the relationships between the emphasis on rule-oriented adjudication in the legal system and the development of markets as the predominant form of exchange.

NORMATIVE ISSUES

"Opting Out" of the Social Contract

Given the existence of a variety of background institutions that make possible various forms of economic exchange, given the fact that these institutions are often not chosen voluntarily by the members of a society (we are confronted by them, rather than having chosen them), and given the difficulty in making fundamental changes in these institutions, the traditional problem of justification arises. Why must we conduct ourselves according to the requirements of such institutions and accept the various obligations and duties that arise? This is the problem that Professor Thomas Scanlon, a philosopher from Princeton University, deals with in his paper. He argues that the framework within which such issues are best discussed is that of social contract theory—in particular, the hypothetical version argued for most forcefully in recent years by John Rawls (1971). If institutions to which we cannot meaningfully be said to have actually consented are to be justified, it should be in terms of arguments about the choices of rational agents under certain specified conditions. The nature of the conditions will be determined in part by our views of what choices are fair and in part by our views of what choices ought to be made.

The particular rules Scanlon is chiefly concerned with are those specifying the obligations of individuals to contribute to society (how much, in what form, and who makes the decision). At one extreme would be a system in which obligations are assumed only by the making of voluntary contracts; at the other would be one in which obligations are completely independent of the individuals' decisions. Obviously, no actual system corresponds to these extremes. The important theoretical question is to provide a framework within which one could evaluate various "mixes."

The possibility of members of a given society "opting out" of the existing institutional arrangements and bargaining as free agents with the remaining members of the society poses both practical and theoretical problems for societies with major nonmarket institutions. The practical problem is that such societies will be unstable and continually subject to defection by their most talented members. The theoretical problem, within the framework of consent theory, is that there may be no argument that it is rational for such members to consent to the institutions of the society. Scanlon argues that there is a way in which we can justify the choice of certain restraints on market institutions to all parties concerned, by appealing to the relative weight of the competing interests at stake: the most talented may have to forego the opportunity to extract the maximum benefit from one's talents so that some other members will not have to come under the domination of those who control the goods necessary for life in their society.

Initial Endowments and Final Inequalities

Proceeding from the idea of a market as an institution that presupposes certain premarket conditions, James Buchanan, an economist from Virginia Polytechnic Institute and State University, deals with the issue of initial inequalities in endowments among the participants in a market economy. Individuals differ in preferences and in various talents and abilities. As a result, even in a system of equality of opportunity and of political power, final distribution of goods and services will vary widely from individual to individual. There is much political pressure to equalize, in some fashion, final distribution—with the State as the usual mechanism. In Buchanan's view, this creates a tension between political equality among persons (with its leveling tendencies) and the desire to limit the encroachment of the State on private action.

Buchanan states that those who blame the market for bad distributive results ought in fact to be blaming the premarket distribution of endowments among persons. By setting up two idealized models (in one, holding preferences constant, in the other, holding endowments constant) Buchanan argues that there is no legitimate basis for prohibiting or restricting market exchange, given the assumption that individual preferences are to be satisfied and that externalities (impacts on others that cannot be charged to their originators) are absent. But Buchanan goes beyond the traditional economic argument that government intervention in the market process worsens the position of all parties. The traditional view, that distributional policy should be handled by direct transfers without interfering with the market, opens the possibility for unlimited leveling. Hence, a certain degree of hypocrisy may be useful: By attacking the market, politicians may both obscure the conflicts that arise from differences in premarket endowments and, by creating the appearance of action, reconcile the public to inequalities in distribution that might be abolished by more direct transfer schemes.

The questions of differences in endowments is receiving increasing attention as scientific evidence is accumulated about the nature and extent of individual differences along various dimensions. Whatever the final picture, it is quite clear, and has long been recognized on a common-sense level, that people are only approximately natural equals. How this fact connects with views of political and economic equality, with institutions of private property and individual rights to accumulate goods, with differential rewards (whether expressed in monetary terms or in those of prestige and status), is perhaps the crucial political issue facing us.

Leisure versus Consumption in Market Economies

Gerald Cohen, a philosopher from the University of London, writing from a Marxian perspective, discusses a rather different tension that he believes is inherent in advanced capitalist societies. While there is some dispute among economists as to whether firms seek to maximize profit or growth, there is agreement that firms must aim at maximizing some combination of these two goals. Hence, there is a constant emphasis on increasing productivity. Improvements in productivity can be used to increase output with constant labor time, decrease labor while maintaining constant output, or some combination of the two. Cohen argues that there is a tendency inherent in advanced capitalism to promote output expansion rather than labor reduction, since only the former promotes profit and competitive strength. As a result, there is a constant tendency to promote increased consumption as well. We have then the paradox that the economic system most able to relieve unpleasant and undesired labor is least willing to do so. Another premise in this argument is that at some point it is irrational not to trade off some consumption for a reduction in the amount of labor time expended. The conclusion is that advanced capitalism, in its American manifestation, behaves in an irrational manner.

A number of questions arise about the concept of work used in Cohen's argument. Is *work*, by definition, something that people would prefer to do less (or none) of? What activities can be considered labor: traveling to work; shopping for food; housework?

There are also problems about the nature of the claim that capitalism *tends* to produce a certain effect. How does one go about testing hypotheses about tendencies? And what is the significance of the fact that noncapitalist societies may manifest the same results but for rather different reasons—having to do, say, with the political, as opposed to the economic structure?

Income Redistribution: Cash or Kind

Lester Thurow, a Massachusetts Institute of Technology economist, takes up a narrower and more technical issue: the relative advantages of in-kind versus cash transfers for income redistribution. The traditional economist's argument is that cash is always more efficient (as defined earlier) than in-kind transfers, since the recipient who desires the in-kind good can always purchase it, and if he doesn't desire it, is better off with the cash. But if the giver derives satisfaction from the recipient having a particular good (whether it be food, housing, or education, etc.) then the issue of which form of gift is more efficient is complex and will depend on various empirical assumptions.

Thurow makes a distinction between two different kinds of preferences: those concerning what economic rules would be best from an ideal point of view and those that concern the maximization of utility within any given economic system. The former are called *individual societal preferences* and the latter, *private-personal preferences*. Notions, such as equality of opportunity or freedom of contract, express individual societal preferences about the form a society should take. If, for example, a society wants to have equality in the distribution of medical care while permitting inequality in the distribution of other goods and services, then in-kind distribution of medical services would be the rational way to proceed. Alternatively, if the society wishes to equalize educational consumption, but not to prescribe in a detailed way the nature of that educational consumption, a voucher system would be the most rational.

Of course, other values complicate matters. If we are interested only in literacy, then educational vouchers might be superior to the provision of public schools. But if we are interested in exposing all children to a set of basic values held by the community, then the reverse preference is rational.

Thurow concludes that there is no correct theorem that cash transfers are superior to restricted transfers of various kinds, but he does think that the basic reasons in favor of not interfering with the expenditure decisions of individuals are strong enough to establish that the burden of proof falls on those who advocate restricted grants.

Since one of Thurow's points is that an economic system does not simply satisfy existing wants but also, directly and indirectly, generates wants, the issue of true versus false needs and desires is raised. What role does advertising play in the creation of demand? Is it merely the tapping of existing demands or does it create new desires? If it does, is there anything wrong with this? Can one draw a principled distinction between "real" and "artificial" wants? Can one do this in purely formal terms (i.e., in terms of how the wants are generated) or must one refer to substantive questions (the question of "human nature")? What beliefs are so fundamental in the society that we do not want to leave it to the accidental forces of the marketplace to determine whether individuals are exposed to them?

HEALTH CARE

An Argument for the Free Market in Medicine

The final session of the Battelle conference was given over to a consideration of the practical impact and moral status of marketplace mechanisms in the delivery of health care services. Obviously, the United States faces a major decision regarding the extent to which health care delivery should be accomplished through planned government programs rather than through the operation of marketed private medicine. All can agree that health is a precious resource, but there is a great debate about whether the State would be wise, or is obliged, to provide tax-supported health care services to all of its citizens.

University of Chicago economist Reuben Kessel, who tragically died before this book went to press, provides a set of arguments, claiming that there has been *too little* free enterprise in the field of medicine, rather than too much, as is often supposed and argued. One example is in the field of medical education, which Kessel believes provides too few physicians to the society because of unnecessary restrictions on the number of available positions and the means of operation within medical schools. He attributes the current situation to the enormous impact of the 1910 Flexner Report on American Medicine and Medical Education. This report, heralded by many as the beginning of truly modern medical practice in America, has had, in Kessel's view, the unfortunate effect of strangling innovative or low-cost means of medical education. Another result appears to have been that the frequency of blacks receiving medical education in the United States was sharply curtailed when the impact of the Flexner Report caused five of the seven black medical shools operating before 1910 to be closed. Similarly, the number of women in medical education was markedly reduced after the report. It was not until 1940 that the number of women in American medical education once again reached its pre-1910 level.

Professor Kessel advances an argument along similar lines in regard to the distribution of blood. He discounts the often-heard argument that blood undersupply and hepatitis-tainting are due to the commercialization of blood banking. Instead, he maintains, it is inadequate commercial safeguards that lead to these problems. Blood is one of the only remaining important products on the market to be sold under virtual *caveat emptor* conditions. This has not been due directly to lack of judicial concern for the equities involved, for courts in at least five states have held hospitals and blood banks strictly liable in tort when patients suffering from transfusion hepatitis have brought suit. However, these decisions have brought about large and successful lobbying campaigns by the American Red Cross and other blood suppliers to protect them from product liability.

Thus, in the current state of affairs, suppliers of blood are not held to the same commercial standards as their commercial neighbors, the pharmaceutical companies.

The Gift of Blood

A rejoinder to Kessel's view is provided by philosopher Peter Singer of New York University. Drawing on the English experience with voluntary blood distribution that has been summarized and analyzed by Richard Titmuss (1970), Singer argues that there are both medical and altruistic reasons to support voluntary, as opposed to commercial, banking of blood. To begin with, of course, the commercial blood donor, often moved to sell blood by dire financial necessity, is more likely than the volunteer to be ignorant or deceitful in regard to his history of hepatitis or venereal disease. Were there a fail-safe assay procedure for hepatitis in serum, then the argument against using the commercial donor would be weakened, at least on technical grounds, but no such assay has been developed yet. Of course there is validity to Kessel's argument that product liability legislation would cause blood procurers to be very selective in choosing their donors; but along with this selectivity would come, inevitably, an increase in product price. In Singer's view, the problem is better solved by moving to the English system of completely voluntary blood giving. In addition to finessing the technical problems, voluntary giving provides for an expression of altruism and the bestowal of a priceless commodity. The values created and maintained by this gift exchange are in themselves so important to the society that they should not be cheapened or threatened by commercial activity.

Obviously, this strong contrast between the views of Kessell and Singer needs to be considered within the framework of the differences that set the United Kingdom and the United States apart in so many dimensions. It might be, for example, that a completely voluntary blood donation program in America would fail to meet the existing demand. Additionally, one needs to weigh the advantages of voluntarism against the disadvantages of State infringement on persons' dispositions of their physical selves.

The Right to Health

Finally, in a paper designed generally to elucidate some of the fundamental issues involved in our concept of health, Charles Fried of the Harvard Law School begins with a critique of the currently fashionable economic theory of rights, in particular, some of the analysis associated primarily with the economist Ronald Coase. Fried points out that the great value of Coase's basic insight (that there is a natural reciprocity in any bargaining situation such that, in a world free of transaction costs, the outcome of pure market bargaining will be maximally efficient) has been pushed beyond its useful limits as a starting place for moral discourse. To begin with, it must be true that rules about bargaining ought not themselves to be subject to the bargaining process envisaged in the Coase theorem; there must be a realm of moral discourse and concern for rights that stands outside the frictionless bargaining process. We have a sensible aversion to the idea of free bargaining about whether lying will be permitted in bargaining. Second, the economic theory is incorrect when it asserts that ethical issues have only to do with norms concerning what people should have in the way of rights, *given* that the mechanism for distribution is the efficient process of free, frictionless bargaining. On the contrary, Fried argues, the questions of distribution of a least some rights may be determined more correctly without reference to the criterion of efficiency. The extent to which people ought differentially to share particular social benefits cannot be derived solely from premises of economic efficiency, with lump sum transfers of cash being used to correct income distribution. It is not generally true that all values and preferences can be traded off smoothly against one another, in even the best of market situations.

These and several related arguments bring Fried to the conclusion that the economic theory of rights fails as a starting place because it is dependent on preconditions that must themselves be the subject of normative discourse. In particular, it seems clear that a moral precondition for bargaining within the market, even a market free of transaction costs, is that the bargainers exist as human selves possessed of a basic sense of self-respect. Self-respect, and even more basically, selfhood, are necessary features of agents who are to bargain morally. And this concept of selfhood is, at the very least, dependent on certain minimal standards of physiological integrity. The self is dependent on the body; a threat to physical well-being is a threat to selfhood. There must be a minimum level or degree of physical health that is required for fair bargaining in the market, and therefore the acquisition of the goods and services required to achieve that minimum level ought not be dependent on market processes. Given that health is a precondition for fair bargaining, it cannot itself be bargained for; it must be provided from without the market structure. Health is a natural right.

SUMMARY

Since Hume, philosophers have called attention to the "logical gap" that separates normative from factual judgments. Formulating social policy requires normative judgments concerning the ends that such policy seeks to attain, the appropriateness of the means used, the type of society we would like to live in, and the values we wish to develop and preserve. Statements about the nature of rational persons, which occur in judgments of economists, philosophers, and psychologists, sometimes represent an attempt to close the gap. Such assertions are both about *how* people do decide and choose and about *what* is rational for them to prefer and choose. Judgments about the use of markets or various command systems to organize production and distribution share this double feature. For such decisions not only reflect our current preferences and desires but, via their implementation, affect in a profound manner the kinds of persons we shall become. To make such crucial decisions, we need to know as much as possible about ourselves and to think as clearly as possible about what we should become. The intersection of economics, psychology, and moral philosophy is a promising place to begin inquiry.

REFERENCES

Calabresi, G. (1970) *The Costs of Accidents.* New Haven, Conn.: Yale University Press.

Coase, R. (1960) "The Problem of Social Cost," in *Journal of Law and Economics,* 3, pp. 1-44.

Musgrave, R. (1959) *The Theory of Public Finance.* New York: McGraw-Hill.

Rawls, J. (1971) *A Theory of Justice.* Cambridge, Mass.: Harvard University Press.

Titmuss, R. (1970) *The Gift Relationship.* London: Allen and Unwin.

2

ABSOLUTIZATION OF THE MARKET: SOME NOTES ON HOW WE GOT FROM THERE TO HERE

BERNARD BARBER
Columbia University

INTRODUCTION AND BACKGROUND

Before presenting a historical sketch of the idea of the market, it will be useful to get some view of where it is now. After all, that is the ultimate goal—improving current understanding of the market and the other forms of social exchange. Looking at the present, one finds the concept that here, exaggerating a little for effect, will be called the *absolutization* of the market. The tendency to absolutization occurs in two interacting contexts, the scientific and the ideological; together they give the concept of the market an intellectual force and polemic urgency that establishes it still as a prime concept, even in a modern world where a great many societies, perhaps a majority, have declared themselves socialist and antimarket.

In the scientific context, the concept of *market* has all the tendency to absolutization, to reification, to the fallacy of misplaced concreteness that established paradigms—as we have come to call them since the publication of Thomas Kuhn's now-classic book (1970)—always have for their adherents and practitioners. The theories and propositions of economic analysis are a magnificent intellectual creation, to be admired no less for their own structure and elegance than for their considerable power in understanding and controlling the real world. Although these theories *assume* a market economy and rationalizing or economizing behavior by the actors in such an economy, these fundamental assumptions tend to be taken for granted, no longer questioned, no longer only possibly one alternative among different types of economy and different types of behavior. So it always is with the fundamental assumptions of highly successful, established scientific paradigms: The greater the success, the more its adherents are blinded to alternatives, and the more they get caught up in the excitement and rewards of extending and refining the established paradigm. This situation of high excitement and high reward has been characteristic of the science of economics for some time now. There are those who point out anomalies, but these are brushed aside, as anomalies tend to be, especially when no new and more successful paradigm is offered. This absolutization of the idea of the market, this tendency to the reification of technical economic analysis that assumes the market, is characteristic of both more liberal and more conservative economists. This shows that to some extent, though not wholly, of course, an established paradigm is more powerful than values and associated ideologies.

So powerful is the scientific concept of the market and its notion of economizing man that it tends not only to be absolutized in its own sphere but even transfered to other areas, to other social science disciplines. Thus we find some psychologists, some political scientists, and some sociologists conceptualizing even their own special aspects of action phenomena as market phenomena. George Homans (1961), for example, has applied "rationalizing" or "market" models to all social behavior. Going in the same direction, but with some apparent qualifications, is another sociologist, Peter Blau (1964). There is, of course, a "rationalizing" aspect to many kinds of behavior other than economic, but this tendency by other social science disciplines to treat their basic material as if it were no different from that of economics would seem to argue more for their admiration of the success of economics than for the likely success of an exclusively market model in their own special spheres. Because of its success, economics is looked to by some in the other social sciences the way physics has been looked to by some in biology.

In our present situation, the idea of the market is also powerful in the ideological context. This is probably the context that European institutional economist Karl Polanyi (1944) referred to in the very important book, *The Great Transformation,* when he spoke several times of "the market utopia." Karl Mannheim (1946), in *Ideology and Utopia,* defined *ideology* as conservative beliefs, justifying the status quo, and *utopia* as revolutionary beliefs, distorting important aspects of reality in order to justify change. Formerly, Polanyi said, the market was a utopia, but now it has become an ideology. The market as ideology is not equally powerful in all quarters. Still, where it is very strong, as in the writings of Milton Friedman or his colleagues at the University of Chicago, it exercises a polarizing and polemic force even for those who do not hold similar beliefs (Friedman, 1962). For example, in Titmuss' *The Gift Relationship* (1971), one can see the author reacting strongly against the market as ideology. In such a reaction he seems to feel a need to deny the market any function at all in the processes of social exchange. With the burden of the market as ideology weighing heavily on him, he must proclaim an ideology of altruistic exchange, which has some of the same tendencies to absolutization as the ideology it is combating. (For a theory of ideology and the tendency toward polarization in ideologies, see Barber, 1971.)

The market as ideology speaks on behalf of a number of different value elements, such as efficiency and equity, but chief among these is the value of freedom. We shall return to the notion of freedom toward the end of this chapter, after a look at the history of how the idea of the market developed. It turns out that freedom has different meanings for different people and that exploring these different meanings can help achieve a better understanding of the various institutionalized processes of social exchange.

HISTORY

The present holds with the market as a powerful idea, more implicitly than explicitly powerful in the scientific context, but explicitly powerful in the ideological context, where the importance of the idea is in no way lessened by its representation as a majority of ideological "anti's" combating a minority of ideological "pro's." There seems to be a general consensus that the market is powerful. Indeed, as with so much that is powerful, it appears that it has always been there, has always been powerful. But this is not so: The history of economic thought shows a suprisingly small amount of attention given to the idea of market. There is a tendency to read the present into the past.[1] The evidence of this unexpected finding and a possible explanation for it follow.

To get a comprehensive perspective, I started with the *International Encyopedia of the Social Sciences (I.E.S.S.)*. Though its list of economics topics had been made up by two distinguished economists, one speaking for economics in general, the other for econometrics more specifically, I found not a single general article on the idea of the market. (Remember that the *I.E.S.S.* prides itself on having general surveys of social science fields and concepts as well as more specific articles.) Wherever *market* was indexed in the *I.E.S.S.*, the reference was to some technical analysis of market structure or process, to concepts such as *perfect monopoly* or *oligopoly*, never to the market as one institutionalized form of social exchange. The only treatment of the market as an institution occurs in anthropologist Helen Codere's 1968 article on "Exchange and Display," which will be discussed later. In sum, it is clear from the contents of the *I.E.S.S.* that economists assume the market to be an institutionalized structure; it is a basic paradigm for them and their "normal science;" they do not raise questions about its fundamental assumptions.

A move from the topical articles in the *I.E.S.S.* to the

biographies of the great figures in the history of economic thought turned puzzlement into conviction and surprise. Even the great figures had said relatively little about the market as such, at least according to articles by Jacob Viner on Adam Smith, Mark Blaug on Ricardo, and, in separate pieces by two sympathetic scholars, Maximilien Rubel and Tom Bottomore on Marx. (It was at this point, I think, that I began testing my finding on my colleagues.)

A final phase of research included important scholarly monographs on some of these figures and to their own works. Since the absence of discussion of the market in Marx was most surprising, I looked at the joint monograph on him by Bottomore and Rubel (1956) and at Paul Sweezy's *The Theory of Capitalist Development* (1942). Again, nothing on the market. Several other books on Marx or collections of his writings had nothing on the market. The three volumes of Marx's *Capital* (1906) itself have only one 10-page chapter on exchange, and in that chapter, the word *market* is used only twice—in passing. Obviously, Marx was interested in many matters bearing on the market, such as the labor theory of value and ownership of the means of production, but of the market itself he says nothing. And the same is true of Adam Smith: His long tome, *An Inquiry into the Nature and Causes of the Wealth of Nations* (1937), mentions the market in only one chapter, entitled "That the Division of Labour is Limited by the Extent of the Market." In this 5-page chapter, it is the division of labor that interests Smith, not the market as a form of social exchange. Even Jean Baptiste Say's so-called "Law of Markets," it turns out on inquiry, was not about the market as a social institution. Say himself did not use the term *market* and simply said that, in exchange, "products are exchanged for products," apparently meaning thereby that everyone participating in a market was better off. This was, of course, contrary to the then-established mercantilist proposition that, in exchange, one gained only what the other lost. In present terminology, Say was asserting the market exchange is not a zero-sum game.

One last piece of evidence for the surprising finding that economic thought has had little to say directly about the market as a social institution: If one looks into Joseph Schumpeter's enormously detailed and immensely scholarly *History of Eco-*

nomic Analysis (1954), one discovers that in all of its 1,200 pages there is no section on "the market" and that "the market" is not even idexed in a subject index that is 30 pages long.

How, then, shall we account for this unexpected finding, the absence of the concept of the market from this history of economic analysis? A full and adequate explanation must be left to others, to those who will take a fresh and intensive look at this history and not just read the present back into the past. For present purposes, I can offer only some suggestions.

The economic theorists and ideologists of the late-eighteenth and nineteenth centuries did not have a vision of the market system that lay in the future or that was coming into being as time passed. It was not for them that explicit, full-blown utopia, as Polanyi (1944) called it when it had already come wholly into being (indeed, when Polanyi felt it had collapsed). Just as the historical process created what we know as the market in a bits-and-pieces, incremental, unintended fashion, so each of the theorists and ideologists among the significant actors in this historical process created only bits and pieces of what gradually coalesced into a highly structured, intellectual creation that had both its scientific and its ideological functions. Somewhere along the way, the term *market* did come to be more and more used; historical scholarship will have to investigate this development. Probably this term was used more by ideologists and policy-makers at first, only later coming into the lexicon of economic theorists. By now, of course, it has become a fundamental assumption of economic theory, though as Schumpeter's (1954) history of economic analysis bears witness, it is a relatively unexamined assumption, more a comprehensive term for the component structures and processes on which economists con-centrate than something they have at the center of their analytical attention.

If one looks to see which social scientists have direct analytic interest in the institution of the market, one sees a European institutional economist such as Polanyi (1944, 1957); a social system sociologist such as Parsons (Parsons and Smelser, 1956); or anthropologists such as Malinowski (1922), Firth (1929), and Codere (1968). All of these social scientists see the market as a type of exchange system that is only one among various alternative structural possibilities. Although there have been some exceptions among economists—for instance, Charles Lindblom's work (Dahl and Lindblom, 1953) on the processes of allocation in social systems—most of them have not devoted their energies and intellectual powers to the market as a system in the way in which they have analyzed its constituent structures and processes. Even in the face of the challenge from those, especially in the socialist world, who have spoken of the efficiency and equity of planning as an economic process, the mainstream economists continue to devote nearly all their attention to the problems set them by their own paradigms and their own ideologies.

We should remember not only that the efforts of the nineteenth-century economists and economic ideologists were of the bits-and-pieces type, but that much of their work was negative. They were not in the happy situation of some present-day sciences, where a new theory—such as the double-helix theory in biology—or some crucial bit of empirical evidence, can quickly, almost immediately, overturn the established scientific paradigm. And we all know that old ideologies die hard, even in the face of massive evidence to the contrary. Economists of the nineteenth century had to criticize, to negate, to disprove the older theories and ideologies. If they talked of the correctness of a new theory of rent as Ricardo did, or of the virtues of the division of labor as Adam Smith (1937) did, or of the values of freedom and laissez-faire as a great many people did, they also had to combat mercantilist economic theories and traditional social ideologies that were not easily given up. Structural changes in society and vast new ideological tides were in their favor, of course, but the history of the times shows how slow and hard social, scientific, and ideological changes were, how the new men—the revolutionaries in ideas and in society—had to fight every inch of the way. Their advances were all hard won. They probably spent more time looking backward at their enemies than forward to some grand new utopian reality. Perhaps it was only when the slow, disordered, bits-and-pieces battle was won that more recent times could afford to think in terms of the utopia of the market.

SOME LESSONS

Is there a lesson for the present in all this? Perhaps it does show more clearly than ever the lack of direct, sustained, and powerful attention by economists to the market as a system and to its various alternatives. There is obviously a need for such attention. That is what economist Charles Kindleberger (1974) meant in his appreciative essay on Polanyi when he said, "*The Great Transformation* is a useful corrective to the economic interpretation of the world and should be read more and more by economists, particularly those of the Chicago school." We need more following up of the work done by Polanyi.

There is still another lesson in this: namely, that it is extremely difficult, even in the face of the evidence presented, for those caught up in the established market paradigm to accept what I have said about present defects in the use of this paradigm. "Marxist" scholars may protest that the notion of the market was really and powerfully present in the writings of Marx, even if only *implicitly*, of course. And scholars of a more "orthodox" economic persuasion have said the same—that the "capitalist" economists were really dealing with the same issues, but not under the heading *market*. I have tried to stress that of course the notion of the market is *implicit* in all kinds of economic theory, both for and against the market. The essential point is that it is of the greatest importance in scientific analysis that implicit assumptions tend not to be questioned and researched if they are not made explicit. The basic characteristics of the market system as a social, institutional, and psychological model must be made completely explicit before both its virtues and its limitations as a paradigm can become the focus of continuing and searching scientific examination and test.

SOME SYSTEMATIC PROBLEMS

Now we will look somewhat more systematically at some of the problems raised by this discussion of the market as a social institution, beginning with some basic notions from the sociology of exchange institutions. Of course, exchange is only one of the economic institutions that a sociology of economics would concern itself with. Structures and processes of production or property and of organization are also essential foci for institutionalization in economic phenomena. After this abbreviated account of exchange institutions, the "embeddedness" problem, the "freedom" problem, and the "integration" problem will be discussed. (Essential references for this whole discussion are Codere, 1968; Firth, 1929; Malinowski, 1922; Parsons and Smelser, 1956; Polanyi, 1944; and Polanyi et al., 1957.)

The Nature of Exchange

Economic exchange is *sui generis*, as it is so often conceived or assumed to be, only in a limited sense. For all kinds of social scientists it is most useful to see economic exchange as only one type of social interaction. All social interaction is governed in part by values and norms. Moreover, each type of social interaction is further constrained by its interdependence with other types. Thus, not only is economic exchange governed by different values and norms in different societies,, but it also has different kinds of interdependence with other types of social interaction, such as those contained in the kinship institutions, or the political institutions, or the stratificational intitutions. As a result of these interdependencies with, or constraints from, both values and other institutional structures, economic exchange can be patterned in different ways. We need to look both at the general problem of what some of these different ways may be an at the specific problem of what the special value and social structural interdependencies are for the market type of economic exchange.

With regard to the general problem of the different ways in which economic exchange can be patterned, theory is not very settled and research is not very extensive. We have seen that the discipline of economics has been engaged elsewhere. It has been anthropologists and sociologists and a few institutional economists who have made some beginnings. Since Karl Polanyi's work represents one such powerful beginning, we can start there. Keep in mind that our purpose is to try to open up the whole problem of the types and functions of different forms of economic and social exchange. We will use Polanyi as a point of reference.

Polanyi has proposed a typology of three kinds of exchange: *reciprocal, redistributive,* and *market.* The reciprocal type of exchange exists when the relevant values and norms prescribe that individuals who are reciprocally obligated to one another by their statuses in any of a variety of particularistic collectivities, such as family, clan, tribe, fealty structures, communities, or friendships, give to and receive from one another in traditionally patterned ways just by virtue of their status relationships. Classic descriptions of concrete examples of reciprocal exchange can be found in Malinowski's (1922) account of how the mother's brother in a matrilineal society like that of the Trobriands in the South Seas has economic exchange relations with his sister and her son or how, in the same area of the world, the men of the Trobriands exchange the ceremonial gifts of necklaces and armbands with their traditional "kula ring" partners in the nearby island. Reciprocal exchange is likely to flourish in societies where particularistic structures such as kinship are the foci for a great deal of social interaction—religious, magic, and political, as well as exchange. Since such particularistic structures have been very important foci for social interaction in all societies throughout the world until modern times, and in many of them still are today, it is clear that historically the reciprocal type of economic exchange has been of prime significance. Further, insofar as particularistic obligations have their place and functions even in a predominantly market economy society— witness the importance of kinship and friendship exchange in our own society—reciprocal exchange is still a type of prime significance for empirical as well as for analytic understanding.

What Polanyi has called *reciprocal exchange* is, of course, pretty much what Marcel Mauss (1925), the French sociologist who worked with anthropological materials, means by *gift exchange.* It is to Mauss rather than to Polanyi that Titmuss in his book, *The Gift Relationship* (1971), expresses his intellectual debt, but his analysis and argument would not have been changed much had he used Polanyi instead of Mauss as an intellectual guide. Titmuss would like to see reciprocal or gift exchange have an enlarged scope in the modern world, because he wants that world to be bound together more by a community solidarity and a community feeling within which reciprocal exchange is more appropriate than market exchange.

In effect, he says he wants all strangers to be brothers, owing each other not only free gifts of untainted blood, but, presumably, exchanges of whatever else man needs for his well-being. Though there is not so much as Titmuss would like, there is perhaps more of reciprocal exchange in the modern world than some have noticed. It would be a useful exercise to look at those areas where kin, friendship, and community obligations persist and calculate the amount of value in other terms of the reciprocal exchange that we often ignore or even sneer at.

Polanyi's second type, *redistributive exchange*, exists where the values or norms prescribe that members of a collectivity—local, national, or even imperial—make contributions of taxes or goods or services to some central agency, which has the responsibility of allocating these contributions to some common enterprise of the collectivity or of returning them in somewhat different measure and in somewhat different proportions to the original donors. While the structures and processes of redistributive exchange are probably clearest in the taxes that members of large national or imperial collectivities pay so that the central agency can pursue the public welfare, in somewhat less sharp outline, redistributive exchange can be seen in any society where the division of labor is great enough and the public interest sufficiently supraindividual so that some central agency is required to collect adequate individual resources to make the public enterprises possible. Thus, there is something of redistributive exchange in the community fishing enterprises that Malinowski (1922) describes in the Trobriands. There seems to be something of redistributive exchange, as well as reciprocal exchange, in the Northwest Coast American Indian potlatches which have fascinated anthropologists and layman alike (Rosman and Rubel, 1971). Certainly, there was redistributive exchange in what have been called the *hydraulic empires* of ancient Egypt and China. And, of course, in the modern world, not only in what are called *welfare societies*, but even in centers of capitalism like the United States, there is a great deal of redistributive exchange. It is interesting that Titmuss, with his own form of noble utopianism, seems to neglect redistributive exchange and concentrate on reciprocal and market exchange, praising the former and damning the latter.

There is, finally, *market exchange*. In this type of exchange the values and norms prescribe that each of the role partners in the interaction must behave like what has been called *homo economicus*, that is, as an economizing, rationalizing individual—considering only price, buying cheap and selling dear, treating all buyers and sellers on the market impersonally and honestly. While there has sometimes been a tendency to psychologize this notion of homo economicus, to treat it as a class of motives, to assume that when Adam Smith (1937) spoke of "man's propensity to truck, barter, and exchange," he was imputing biological instincts or psychological motives rather than speaking merely descriptively, it is essential to understand that market exchange behavior in the relevant situations is prescribed by values and norms, regardless of motivation, and that it depends for its possibility on a definite set of institutional arrangements. Thus, the great sociologists from Durkheim forward have stressed the institution of contract, what Durkheim called the "non-contractual element in contract," as an indispensable component of market exchange structures and processes. Market exchange works only if honesty is institutionalized and further supported, if either confusion of understanding or deviance occur, by a whole institutionalized law of contract. Maine had hold of a central sociological fact when he asserted that previous societies had been societies of *status* and that the modern world was a world of *contract*. Status prescribes reciprocal and redistributive types of exchange; contract prescribes the market.

Market exchange is interdependent, of course, with a set of modern values and social structures: equity, efficiency, mobility of person and group, widespread education, certain rules of property, a government that is willing to regulate the economy just far enough to make the market viable and no farther, and so forth. There is no need here to go into all this in detail. Some of this analysis exists already. What is needed is more systematic analysis, based on empirical research; of course, this should be part of the larger enterprise of doing the same analysis and research for the other forms of economic exchange. Only out of this would come the scientific knowledge of economic exchange as a type of social interaction that is needed for better scientific analysis and better policy relevance.

One thing does seem clear from what we have said about the

types of economic exchange: The modern world has a mix of all three types, perhaps because each does have some place in the different sets of values and structures that make up modern societies and the larger world. More science and less ideology in the discussion of economic exchange might clarify what the proper places and proper mixes of the different types are or could be in different societies and in the world as a whole.

The "Embeddedness" Problem

A few words now about the problem of what Polanyi et al. (1957) call the "embeddedness" or "disembeddedness" of the various types of economic exchange institutions. Polanyi describes the market as disembedded, the two other forms of exchange as more embedded with regard to the other social institutions in society. For reasons that are perhaps clear after what has just been said about the sociology of exchange institutions, this is a somewhat misleading image. While the modern market economy could be viewed as somewhat more structurally differentiated, somewhat more concretely separate, from the other institutional subsystems of society, this image diverts attention from the basic sociological fact that all types of exchange institutions are interdependent with their environing value patterns and other institutional subsystems. Market exchange is no less interdependent with its social environment than are reciprocal and redistributive exchange. Calling market exchange *disembedded* leads attention away from analyzing just how it is interdependent with the other parts of its societal system; it gives it a false kind of analytical, as well as concrete, independence. From these errors come further errors, such as the belief that the other institutions and values are wholly dependent on, rather than interdependent with, a market economy. There is neither structural isolation nor analytical independence for any of the types of economic exchange.

The "Freedom" Problem

The "freedom" problem has been a focus of ideological attention in the modern world—*freedom* both in its general meanings and, more specifically, in connection with the market form of exchange. The various meanings of *freedom* must be carefully scrutinized by social scientists, however, since there may be different meanings, both at different times and for those who favor one or another of the different types of economic exchange. In the nineteenth century, of course, when the theorists and ideologists for market exchange were seeking to overturn old values and old social institutions, the freedom slogan took on a very wide scope. They wanted freedom of land, freedom of labor, freedom of capital, freedom of contract, freedom of whatever was necessary to make national and international markets possible for the first time. Although sometimes they seemed utopian, as Polanyi (1944) has alleged, and demanded a kind of absolute freedom, in fact they recognized that there were necessary limits on freedom, that too much freedom would make markets impossible. Early on, for example, they recognized that some kinds of freedom led inevitably to monopoly and the death of markets. They wanted freedom, then, to the degree necessary to make markets possible; they favored government regulations in the specifics that were necessary toward this end. But they opposed governmental regulation in general because it was inconsistent with their general value and ideology of freedom.

At present, however, the ideologists for freedom seem to have a more limited definition. The older battles for free land, labor, and capital have been largely won. There have been fundamental transformations of our social institutions to make all this possible. Now it is governmental regulation that is viewed as the chief, and perhaps sole, infringer on freedom. An economist like Milton Friedman, in his more ideological statements, is a leading spokesman for this point of view (1962, XIII).

But Titmuss, who wishes for reciprocal exchange in a universe where even all strangers are brothers, has a different definition of freedom. He feels that the market entails a loss of all kinds of important freedoms and says explicitly (1971, p. 240) that the loss of these freedoms is not recognized in Friedman's *Capitalism and Freedom*. The freedom he wishes to see men have is, he says,

> the freedom of men not to be exploited in situations of ignorance, uncertainty, unpredictability, and captivity; not to be excluded by market forces from society and from giving relationships, and not to

be forced in all circumstances—and particularly the circumstances described in this study—to choose always their own freedom at the expense of other people's freedom. (p. 242)

Notice, as he constructs his own utopia (*utopia* in the sense of Mannheim, 1946) of universal brotherhood, how he is as much concerned to criticize the negative side of what he defines as "the older order," the market, as he is to stress the positive side of reciprocal, or "altruistic" exchange. (On the interdependence of positive and negative elements in ideologies, see Barber, 1971.)

It is clear that the various types of social and economic exchange do have consequence for the meanings and structures of freedom. Wherever freedom is a value, then, it behooves us to have as good a scientific understanding as we can get of the many forms and consequences of exchange.

The "Integration" Problem

There is, finally, the "integration" problem—the problem of how the market system itself and the larger society of which it is a part maintain some minimally essential degree of order, or equilibrium, or viability. In the nineteenth century, economic theorists and ideologists either assumed or argued that the "hidden hand" of self-regulating processes on the market assured its viability. There was little concern for the integration problem at the level of the larger society. These days, of course, technical economic theory has much more to say about the problems and processes of integration at the market system level, but it still has little to say about societal integration, even insofar as this is vitally affected by the market.

Social scientists from other disciplines, in sharp contrast, have taken the integration problem as central in both the scientific and the moral contexts. There is not space or perhaps need here to tell this story in detail. But we can refer to some of its highlights. Maine, on the consequences of the movement from a society of status to a society of contract, and Tonnies, on the differences and consequences of *gemeinschaft* and *gesellschaft* societies, are two important contributors to the discussion of the problem of integration. Probably the most important figure, however, is Durkheim, for whom the problem of integration is a central scientific and moral concern. His theoretical and empirical discussion of societal integration and its condition of relative absence, *anomie*, in *Le Suicide*, is one of the great classics of social science. And in contemporary social science, Talcott Parsons has aroused great admiration in many quarters for his highly theoretical and systematic analysis of the problems of social integration. It has been his central concern during nearly 50 years of work in sociological theory. Parsons tried explicitly to relate the problem of societal integration with that of market system integration (Parsons and Smelser, 1956), but there has been all too little response and generally not very much interest in this matter on the part of economists. For both scientific and value reasons, there ought to be.

CONCLUSION

Little is needed by way of conclusion. I hope this brief discussion of the history of the idea of the market has illuminated current discussions of exchange phenomena. It should be evident that social scientists can profit from addressing themselves directly and intensively to the nature and functions of the different forms of exchange. A better understanding in this area will help them to say what mix of these different forms will best serve the public welfare in different societies. Value and interest conflicts always remain, of course, but a little more light from a little more social science will surely be useful.

NOTE

1. I should like to stress that I had expected to find the history of economic thought full of discussions of the idea of the market. As I went through some of the literature, I was so suprised to find practically no discussion at all that I began to test my finding with knowledgeable colleagues. All of them said, yes, they would have expected to find a lot and, yes they were surprised that I had found so little. This is what I mean when I say I think we have read our present into our past.

REFERENCES

Barber, B. (1971) "Function, Variability, and Change in Ideological Systems," in B. Barber and A. Inkeles, eds., *Stability and Social Change.* Boston: Little Brown.

Blau, P. (1964) *Exchange and Power in Social Life.* New York: Wiley.

Bottomore, T. B., and Rubel, M., eds. (1956) *Karl Marx: Selected Writings in Sociology and Social Philosophy.* London: Watts.

Codere, H. (1968) "Exchange and Display," in *International Encyclopedia of the Social Sciences.* New York: Macmillan.

Dahl, R. A. and Lindblom, C. E. (1929) *Politics, Economics and Welfare.* New York: Harper.

Firth, R. (1929) *Primitive Economics of the New Zealand Maori.* New York: E. P. Dutton.

Friedman, M. (1962) *Capitalism and Freedom.* Chicago: University of Chicago Press.

Homans, G. (1961) *Social Behavior: Its Elementary Forms.* New York: Harcourt Brace.

Kindleberger, C. P. (1974) "*The Great Transformation* by Karl Polanyi," *Daedalus,* Winter, 45-52.

Kuhn, T. S. (1970) *The Structure of Scientific Revolutions* (2nd ed.). Chicago: University of Chicago Press.

Malinowski, B. (1922) *Argonauts of the Western Pacific.* New York: E. P. Dutton.

Mannheim, K. (1946) *Ideology and Utopia.* New York: Harcourt Brace.

Marx, K. (1906) *Capital* (3 vols.). S. More and E. Aveling, trans.). Chicago: Charles H. Kerr.

Mauss, M. (1925) *The Gift* (I. Cunnison, trans.). London: Cohen and West.

Parsons, T. and Smelser, N. J. (1956) *Economy and Society.* Glencoe, Ill.: The Free Press.

Polanyi, K. (1944) *The Great Transformation.* New York: Farrar.

Polanyi, K., Arensberg, C. M. and Pearson, H. W., eds. (1957) *Trade and Market in the Early Empires.* Glencoe, Ill.: The Free Press.

Rosman, A. and Rubel, P. G. (1971) *Feasting with Mine Enemy: Rank and Exchange Among Northwest Coast Societies.* New York: Columbia University Press.

Schumpeter, J. A. (1954) *History of Economic Analysis.* New York: Oxford University Press.

Smith, A. (1937) *An Inquiry into the Nature and Causes of the Wealth of Nations.* New York: The Modern Library.

Sweezy, P. M. (1942) *The Theory of Capitalist Development.* New York: Oxford University Press.

Titmuss, R. M. (1971) *The Gift Relationship.* New York: Pantheon.

THE MORAL PREDICAMENT
OF THE MARKET ECONOMY

WALTER A. WEISSKOPF
Professor of Economics Emeritus
Roosevelt University

MARKETS, MORALS, AND CHRISTIAN ETHICS

The title of this volume, *Markets and Morals*, points to an antinomy that has accompanied the free market from its inception. Market behavior stood in diametrical opposition to the occidental ethical tradition, especially to Christian ethics. Every kind of conduct required by the market was regarded as sin and concupiscence by Christian ethics. The pursuit of riches for its own sake, buying cheap and selling dear, "cornering the market," and similar practices were morally condemned; so was the uninhibited pursuit of economic self-interest. All this conflicted with the Christian virtues of charity and compassion.

This conflict between ethics and market behavior has survived up to the present and leads to questions discussed here. Academic and popular thought have, during the last two centuries, tried to solve this conflict by interpreting conduct required by the market as virtuous and in line with Christian beliefs and by trying to prove that such behavior promotes the common good.

The first kind of reasoning is found in the work and success ethics of the Protestant Calvinist and Puritan traditions. Economic success was interpreted as a sign that those who acquired riches had been blessed by the Lord. This, in a way, was the first step in changing the evaluation of the profit motive: rather than being a sin, it became a sign of salvation.

However, economic success was also believed to be the result of the virtues of "worldly asceticism;" of postponed gratifications; of impulse control; of hard, persistent, systematic work, thrift, and savings; and rejection of luxurious consumption—in general, of "avoidance of all enjoyment." The bourgeois style of life was thus sanctified by religious beliefs. The profit-seeking entrepreneur was allowed to have a good conscience; justification was also provided for inequalities between rich and poor. The poor were those not chosen to be saved and not chosen to thrive; but it was—and still is, according to this tradition—believed that the poor also lacked the strength of character to practice the bourgeois virtues. By seeing economic success as a mark of salvation, the gap between Christian ethics and market behavior was bridged. Thus, markets and morals in the Western world were made compatible with the help of Christian religion.

THE HISTORICAL CONSEQUENCES

In the nineteenth century, this belief system was severed from religion. Economic success became separated from divine blessing, although this element has never vanished completely from popular thinking; the rich and successful are still regarded, and regard themselves, as somehow superior to others. The basis for this superiority, however, was not found anymore in religion but in natural selection: The rich were the fittest who survived in the struggle for existence, a Darwinian idea (Galbraith, 1958; Hofstadter, 1955).

Puritanism and social Darwinism justified *individual* market behavior. Classical economics, in the formulation of Adam Smith, justified the goals of the market economy as a whole

(Weisskopf, 1973). Smith presented a model of an economic order with the acquisitive attitude as its cornerstone. He justified this economic order by assuming the essential interdependence of (1) individual economic self-interest, (2) the free competitive market, and (3) the common good of society. His idea of the natural harmony of individual economic interests justified individual economic liberty by asserting that a free competitive market would promote the common good through the famous invisible hand. It is of utmost importance to realize that the father of economics justified *individual* economic freedom from the *social* point of view; individual economic freedom is desirable because it accomplishes the *common* economic good. This leads to the reverse conclusion that such freedom is not desirable when its results run counter to the common good.

Adam Smith, and after him many chambers of commerce, tied economic liberty to the profit motive. To legitimize this motive he interpreted the drive for more and more money, wealth, and possessions as a natural trait, a part of nature. He also identified the freedom to acquire more and more with freedom as such, thereby laying the foundation for the identification of the free competitive market, individualism, and democracy, which play such a prominent role in the teachings of the Chicago School of Economics and in the pronouncements of politicians and businessmen. This ideology attributed to the free enterprise system a socially beneficial character and thus justified it morally; it eliminated the antinomy of markets and morals. Acquisitive, competitive man could pursue his economic "egoism" with the assurance that, *nolens volens*, he was promoting the public good. He could strive for profits without guilt feelings.

Another link between market behavior and moral precepts was forged by the labor theory of value in the formulation of the classical economists (but not in the formulation of Marx). If one abstracts from logical problems and considers ethical foundations of this theory, it appears to correspond to the labor and work ethic: Incomes and prices are morally justified as far as they reward individual effort. Those independent producers who work longer and more intensively produce a larger, more valuable product and thus increase their income. Higher incomes and prices are the reward for quantitatively and qualitatively greater effort. This is the original formulation of the slogan: to each according to his productive contribution.

All these beneficial and morally just results were allegedly brought about by the free, self-regulating, competitive market in which prices, wages, and incomes were driven by competition to a just and fair level, and which leads to the production of a maximum national product. In such a system, all participants will feel that they perform a meaningful function and receive a fair share, and that they promote their own and society's welfare by pursuing their economic self-interest. They want more and more, and so does society. Individual and social goals are in harmony, and so are markets and morals.

This classical creed, still alive today in public opinion, succeeds in its moral justification of the free market system only because it rests on an implicit assumption about the identity of individual and social economic goals: They both aim at an ever increasing volume of goods for the nation and for the individuals. Adam Smith defined individual and social interest in the same way, as increase in production. This enables his followers to argue away all possible conflicts of interests between society and individuals. As soon as one recognizes that there can be other interests than the increase in the volume and variety of goods and services (e.g., a more equal distribution or the protection of the environment or noneconomic goals), the concept of the natural harmony of interests and with it the moral justification of the competitive market breaks down. However, in early capitalism the increase in productive and in the production of goods was the predominant problem, and thus the classic creed provided an appropriate moral justification for the market.

THE ABANDONMENT OF MORALS IN ECONOMICS

During the second half of the nineteenth century, this belief in the harmony of markets and morals was translated into "scientific" language by neoclassical economists. In this process, the moral aspects of the creed were almost completely obliterated by subjectivistic hedonism and formal rationalism (Weisskopf, 1973). The idea that the maximization of gains and profits is the supreme individual and social goal of the economy was reinterpreted. In Adam Smith's formulation, this was understood to mean the concrete goal of an increase in the production of goods. It also implied the moral obligation of doing productive work and of observing the rules of conduct prescribed in *Poor Richard's Almanac.*

In neoclassical and marginalist economics, these moral concepts were abandoned (Weisskopf, 1973). It was assumed that the economy did not serve any common good or public interest but merely the satisfaction of individual, subjective preferences based on desires and tastes, mostly directed toward material comforts. These preferences supposedly found their expression in consumers' demands on markets which, in turn, called forth the required supply of goods. The main justification of the free market system was now found in subjective need satisfaction. The moral aspect, prominent in the classical economic creed, was reduced to the formal rationality of the behavior of the marketers. Whatever subjective goal was pursued in a rational, efficient, systematic fashion was assumed to be right. Formal, value-empty rationality for its own sake became the moral philosophy of economics. The link between markets and morals was destroyed. The element of virtue, so strong in the work and success ethics, was reduced to rational pursuit of gain and of sensuous material comforts. In the words of Lionel Robbins: "So far as we economists are concerned our economic subjects can be pure altruists, pure ascetics, pure sensualists" and "individual valuations . . . are from the point of view of economic analysis . . . the irrational element in our universe of discourse" (Robbins, 1946). This provided no moral basis for the legitimation of market behavior.

The development from substantial concrete values to a value-neutral and value-empty interpretation of the economy fitted into a general trend of Western history. Value relativism was accompanied by the disintegration of traditional morality, by the liberation from sensual and sexual repression, and by individualistic subjectivism. The belief in a realm of ideas and ideals, a realm of the *unum verum et bonum*, the one, the true, and the good, the belief in objective intuitive reason that can grasp the essence of things and deal with the individual and social good was abandoned. Reason became technical, instrumental, concerned merely with means for ends assumed to be beyond the pale of reason. This shift in the meaning of reason made impossible any rational discussion about the common good; values, ideals were removed from the realm of reason. Applied to economics, this meant that morals were completely divorced from markets and that one could talk about the goal of the economy only in terms of the maximization of individual preferences. No basis was left for a discussion of the common good except in terms of individual satisfactions.

This separation of markets and morals was supported by a formulation of the laissez-faire philosophy that removed all normative moral elements from economics. As long as self-interest and public interest were found in the production of more goods, and as long as the work ethic was still an implicit part of economic attitudes, the free market system could be accepted as socially beneficial. Because of the growing productive capacity and because of growing affluence, however, the emphasis in economics and in the economy shifted from production to consumption. The problem of the affluent economies was and is not to *produce* more and more goods but to *sell* them. Subjective consumers' experiences became the focus of attention. The economic system promoted the spirit of value-relativistic hedonism, which fitted into the philosophical orientation of modern Western thought. The enjoyment of sensuous consumption experiences was legitimized by intellectual trends; but it was also a goal that met the objectives of the market. The capital-rich Western economies with their tremendous productive capacity required continuous increase of consumers' demands, which were stimulated by the relentless creation of desires through advertising and salesmanship. The goal of rising standards of living through continuous stimulation of desires became necessary for full employment of all material and human resources. The economic system became inseparably tied to subjective, materialistic, sensuous hedonism.

ECONOMIC MEANINGLESSNESS
AND ECONOMIC GROWTH

This situation—the result of a century-long development—led to the point where the moral basis for market behavior disintegrated. The mere earning of an income for the acquisition of increasing creature comforts can be experienced as a social necessity or as a pleasurable game; but it lacks a moral basis and, thus, a meaning. An economic system requires a moral philosophy that makes it meaningful, legitimate, and just. Today the question of markets versus morals arises again because the beliefs that justified our economic system have disintegrated. The Puritan work and success ethic has broken down under the impact of secularization. Laboring for success has lost its religious and moral basis and has become a meaningless end in itself, a mere striving for power and comforts without ethical content. Work had also received a meaning from creativity: giving birth to a useful and beautiful object, creating an environment geared to the human person. It satisfied the "instinct of workmanship." This type of work has been eliminated from the industrial economy under the impact of modern technology with its division of labor. Human skill, supervision, and even decision making are replaced by machines that provide not only the brawn but also the brain necessary in production.

The work process itself has become meaningless, but so has its alleged aim, the earning and spending of an income. For all of us, earning and spending have become necessities; but we have internalized the goal of earning an ever-increasing amount of money and spending it on an ever-increasing volume and variety of goods and services. The imperative of "economic growth" has become a directive for individuals and for society. This has contributed to the meaninglessness of economic life and to the destruction of its moral roots.

In early capitalism, with an economy of relative scarcity, the idea of ever-rising standards of living had a meaning and some moral justification. In the capital-rich, affluent society of the twentieth century, ever-increasing standards of living do not make sense, either for the individual or for society. The wisdom of past ages knew that moderation, and not excesses, in physical need satisfaction is required for health and happiness. Purely on psychological grounds, the ideal of continuously rising standards of living become senseless once a certain standard of subsistence and comfort is reached. A balanced way of life, not excessive economic growth, is a psychologically desirable goal.

This conclusion is reenforced in our time by ecological

dangers. Economists and ecologists become more and more aware of the limits to industrial growth imposed by raw material shortages, pollution, and waste absorption, and of the necessity to preserve the essentials for life in terms of clean air and water. Both—psychological wisdom and ecological knowledge—raise doubts about the traditional economic orientation toward more and more, and thus revive the questions of markets and morals. Morality is concerned with the good of the individual and of society. Ecology is concerned with the biological, physiological bases of life. From both points of view, the market system as it is structured today leads to too many "bad" results. What is necessary is a reorientation of our economic attitudes and goals under the aegis of social and individual morality and of ecology.

The traditional economic growth ideology is mainly supported by big business, big government, big labor, and by their bureacracies. Ironically, these use the free enterprise ideology to justify this goal; but the present economic order is a far cry from the economy of independent producers ruled only by the free market. The unrestricted power of huge organizations is not identical with the economic liberty envisaged by Adam Smith.

There is a growing recognition, however, that the invisible hand of the market has been replaced by the visible hand of corporate and governmental bureaucracies. This makes the question about the relations between markets and morals much more urgent. As long as it is believed that the invisible hand of the market leads to beneficial social results, the question of morality of the market is avoided. In the free market, the invisible hand makes all decisions and choices; nobody is supposed to have any market power. If the visible hand of governmental and corporate bureaucracy guides the economy, questions of goals, values, ends, morals, and meaning of economic activity arise. What can the visible hand of corporations and governments do? What standards should guide the decisions of these organizations? In other words, as long as it is believed that only impersonal market forces guide the economy, no moral decisions have to be made. The striving for profit maximization is all that is required of firms and individuals. But if there is market power, if corporate executives and government bureaucrats are making deliberate choices and decisions that influence everybody's life, there must be guiding norms for such decisions. Neither profit maximization nor the balancing of individual and group interests will suffice; they have led to too many harmful results. A new search for the individual and common good will have to be instituted, and economic decisions must be subject to the new economic morality.

CONCLUSION

Cultural, psychological, ecological, and economic trends point toward the necessity for a normative discipline of economics which, once again, should become a part of "moral philosophy." Neither free competition nor governmental planning alone can fulfill the need for a new economic ethos. Such an ethos must rest on the convictions and beliefs of the people who compose the corporate and governmental bureaucracies and on the spirit of the people who buy their goods and services. This morality can only be pointed to; it cannot be blue-printed. It has to emerge from the grassroots, nurtured by leadership. It will have to be much less acquisitive and less growth-oriented than in the past. More emphasis will have to be put on quality of life than on quantity of goods. People will have to aim at a target income and learn to know when more may become too much. Non-economic activities using up fewer resources will have to replace wasteful activities. The emphasis must be on durability not on obsolescence, and on the preservation of capital and on the stocking of resources instead of their depletion. And above all, noneconomic goals and styles of life will have to move into the center of human existence. Thus, in a way, markets will have to be replaced by morals. This is not a utopian wish but a necessary condition for psychological and physical survival.

REFERENCES

Galbraith, J. K. (1958) *The Affluent Society*. New York: The New American Library.

Hofstadter, R. (1955) *Social Darwinism in American Thought.* Boston: Beacon Press.

Robbins, L. (1946) *An Essay on the Nature and Significance of Economic Science*. London: Macmillan.

Weisskopf, W. A. (1973) *Alienation and Economics*. New York: Delta Books.

4

LIBERTY, CONTRACT, AND CONTRIBUTION

THOMAS M. SCANLON
Princeton University

INTRODUCTION

There is a natural prima facie case for the inclusion of market exchange within any distributive system. For, given any distribution of goods taken as just, if two parties would prefer the result of a bilateral exchange to the status quo why not allow them to trade? Institutions that do not allow or do not provide for such exchanges seem to involve objectionable restrictions on the liberty of those to whom they apply. They appear to be inefficient as well, since each such trade, by moving the trading parties to preferred positions and, we may suppose, leaving others unaffected, moves the whole situation closer to Pareto optimality.

This argument is only prima facie because of several presuppositions only alluded to in this chapter. The first of these is the assumption that no one other than the trading parties is affected by the exchange. As just stated, this is obviously too strong a requirement. Better would be something closer to "no one other than the trading parties is affected in ways one has a right to be protected against." But what are these ways? A whole theory seems to be required to set the threshold of illegitimate interference. A second way of approaching the limitations of the argument, one which may present this problem in a more manageable form, focuses on the justice of the preexisting distribution. If the distribution of goods prior to the exchange is legitimate, then, it would seem, those who hold these goods are entitled to redistribute them as they please. Thus, by appeal to the justice of this distribution (or of the institutions producing it) we may avoid the messy problem of considering and weighing all the possible side effects of each exchange. But this advance is more apparent than real. Virtually any plausible set of institutions will impose some limitations on what one may do with the goods one acquires through the legal forms those institutions specify, and the nature and extent of these limitations is certain to be an important factor in determining the moral acceptability of those institutions. Thus, all the problems involved in setting the threshold of illegitimate interference will reappear in arguments for and against the justifiability of particular sets of institutions and the complexes of rights and limitations they involve.

But there is some advantage in thus pushing the problem one step back—from consideration of the merits of particular transactions to the justification of institutions that allow or limit them. The preference appealed to in the prima facie argument presented above—a preference for the results of exchange over the status quo, given institutions making such exchange possible—does not by itself suffice to establish the preferability of such institutions, even under the assumption that no one other than the trading parties is affected by the transaction. For it is possible that having institutions that allow for transactions of the kind in question involves costs that outweigh the advantages of the opportunity they provide. Arguments by appeal to such costs are in some cases arguments for justifiable paternalism, i.e., claims that the opportunity in question is so likely to be used unwisely that it is rational to prefer not to have this opportunity at all. But to argue against market insititutions by appealing to their costs one need not argue paternalistically. One nonpaternalistic argument is that advanced by Peter Singer (1973, 1977): Having a system in which certain goods and services are exchangeable and can be purchased may foster attitudes toward these goods, toward others, and toward ourselves that one may rationally wish to avoid. The argument I will be considering later in this chapter is also nonpaternalistic, but it does not concern the attitudes and motives engendered by market institutions.

INSTITUTIONS OF VOLUNTARY AGREEMENT

I have so far been concerned with a case for including market exchange within any institution of property, production, and distribution. Markets have been considered as a kind of topping-off mechanism for moving the result of any distributive system closer to Pareto optimality. But market exchange is often conceived as having a more fundamental role. Indeed, the notion of free exchange as represented in the ideal of the market may seem to be *the* fundamental notion of social cooperation. This will seem to be so if one sees such cooperation as freely entered into by individuals who establish the terms of their cooperation through a process of bargaining on the basis of the particular assets—energy, talents, information, and perhaps also transferable goods previously acquired—that they "bring with them." Any other conception of social arrangements, any conception that is not at the fundamental level a market conception will, it may be argued, portray at least some of the participants in social institutions to some degree as unwilling contributors; and, to this degree, the institutions in question must be seen as illegitimate.

But, insofar as it suggests that under ideal market institutions all obligations would derive from specific voluntary undertakings, this argument rests on a mistake. Market institutions themselves—the rules specifying, e.g., how contracts are to be made, that contracts duly made are to be fulfilled, and that contractually acquired property rights are to be respected—cannot derive their authority from particular contracts. Certainly, they do not do so in practice; for persons born into a market society, these institutions and the specific property rights already established under them represent fixed features of social life, factors that apply to them without their consent, constraining and determining the opportunities they will have to enter into truly voluntary arrangements with their contemporaries. The point here is an old one, familiar at lease since Hume. Arguing against attempts to see political authority as founded on a promise by the subjects to obey the sovereign, Hume (1752) contended that such a theory could not account for the obligations of present subjects of existing states, since it was simply not the case that every citizen who was supposed to be obligated could be found to have made such a promise. Further, he argued, the appeal to a promise would, in any case, be theoretically idle, since promising is itself a social institution defined by conventional rules, and the moral requirement of fidelity to that institution (in particular, fidelity to the rule specifying that promises duly made are to be kept) stands just as much in need of philosophical explanation as does the requirement of obedience to political authority.

Now one might argue here, in opposition to Hume, that there is an important sense in which the principle of fidelity to agreements is a natural moral requirement, not dependent on any preexisting social framework. To be sure, two strangers in a state of nature could not exchange *promises* in the strict sense; i.e., they could not invoke our particular institution. But one such person might get another to do something by causing the other to form an expectation of reciprocal service on some specific, future occasion; and the two might even come to an understanding over exactly what conditions attach to this arrangement, e.g., what intervening circumstances would excuse the second party from performance of his part of the bargain. This one encounter hardly makes a social institution, yet it does seem to create a moral obligation. The person who benefits from the first performance is, from a moral point of view, no more free to refuse to perform in turn than he would be had he promised to do so. One might infer from this that the role of a conventionally established system of rules like our institution of promising is merely to serve as an aid in helping us create mutual expectations without having to work out anew, on each occasion, exactly what the form and limits of those expectations are to be. Such an institution has obvious usefulness. Its usefulness increases the motivation to fulfill agreements made under it since people will not want to risk being excluded from its use. But this additional motivation is not essential to the moral force of agreements, which derives from the voluntary creation of mutual expectations.

If this argument is accepted, then Hume's own analysis of the moral basis of fidelity to contracts must be rejected.[1] But something remains of his thesis that promising must be seen as a social institution and appraised as such. Even if the role of social institutions in generating binding agreements is confined to that of providing a ready-made matrix for the formation of mutual expectations, the fact remains that there are many different systems of rules that might fulfill this role. These practices may differ from one another, and from our own institution of promising, in trivial ways, e.g., in the ritual or form of words through which obligations are undertaken, or in more substantial ways, e.g., in the conditions recognized as voiding obligation. If we live in a society in which one of these practices is conventionally established, then, unless we are unusually circumspect and explicit, the provisions of that practice will determine the nature and scope of the obligations we undertake.

But can just any system of rules, or any system that is generally accepted in a community, define morally binding obligations? It seems that there are independent moral requirements which such practices must satisfy. Consider, for example, an institution of "vicarious agreement" according to which some people, say men, could make agreements on behalf of other capable adults, say women, without their consent, and could modify and abrogate agreements already made by them. Such an institution would be morally flawed. Would the fact that it was generally accepted in a society by men and women alike be sufficient to make agreements it sanctions morally binding on women who have not consented to them? Whether this is so will depend, I think, on the nature of this "general acceptance." We would be inclined to regard a woman as morally bound by agreements made in her name only if her acceptance of the institution was not mere acquiescence but of such a nature as to constitute a willing authorization of men to make agreements on her behalf. Given the blanket nature of this authorization, however, it would take clear, positive evidence to convince us that it was freely and knowingly given, as it would have to be to have moral force. Similar remarks would apply to agreements arising from force or fraud under systems of agreement-making that failed to recognize force or fraud as voiding obligations. Such agreements would not in general be morally binding, but it is conceivable that they might be so if the "strict liability" system was something people entered into freely.

These examples all concern moral requirements designed to protect those who make agreements. This is why it seems that these requirements could be set aside by genuine consent. If all moral requirements on systems of agreement-making were of this kind then it might be true, as this discussion has at times suggested, that any agreement is morally binding as long as it is entered into freely by promisor and promisee. But promises can affect third parties. A binding promise creates in the promisee a right which others ought not interfere with. Further, the rights created by a promise can conflict with other claims on the promisor. If I am bound by a promise to help you build your barn tomorrow morning, then I may not be free to help Jones fight his brush fire. If we arrived at our understanding by invoking some social institution of agreement-making, the rules of this institution may provide some guide as to the conditions under which I am released from my obligation because of someone else's claim on me. But a given system of rules may get these conditions wrong, e.g., by specifying that I am bound where in fact I am not. If they do this then the rules are in that respect simply void because they conflict with the relevant moral requirements. These requirements, if they can be set aside at all by voluntary agreement, cannot be amended merely by consent of promisor and promisee. At the very least more general consent would be required.

INSTITUTIONS OF PROPERTY

Much of what I have just said about institutions of voluntary agreement applies *mutatis mutandis* to institutions of property. There are many different ways in which the mechanisms of acquisition and exchange of property, and the rights and prerogatives of property owners, may be constituted. As in the previous case, what our rights as property owners are will, in general, depend on the system of rules conventionally established in our community. And again, as in the previous case, there are moral requirements which these rules must satisfy if the rights and prerogatives they prescribe are to be the basis of legitimate claims under the conditions prevailing in our society. But while the moral limitations on systems of agreement-making that concern effects on third parties are easily overlooked,[2] the corresponding limitations on systems of property are obvious and crucial. To acquire property in an object is to acquire rights that one may press, not only against a particular person with whom one has entered into agreement in order to acquire the property, but also against anyone else who may come along and be in a position to interfere with one's use or disposal of that object. This will include a large number of people with whom the possessor has never come in contact at all. The rights in question therefore exceed the scope of actual face to face agreements.

Now it might be argued here that the obligation not to interfere with the property of others no more needs to be founded on a past agreement than does the obligation not to murder or assult. These are natural moral requirements, which social institutions may make precise and enforce but which they do not create. After all, is it not clear that a person could be wronged by being deprived of his land and crops, even in the absence of any social institutions establishing rights to property? I cannot give a complete answer to this objection here, but I believe that what is violated in cases of the kind just mentioned is not, strictly speaking, a property right. It is rather some general right to noninterference, which covers only a small part of what are usually thought of as property rights. This is shown by the fact that what happens in such an example strikes us as clearly wrong only if we suppose, first, that what is taken is of use to the person from whom it is taken (i.e., that the taking really constitutes an interference with that person's life and activities), and second, that the appropriation and use of this thing by the supposedly wronged party did not already constitute an interference with others, e.g., with the person who did the taking.[3] But in real systems of property (as this notion has generally been understood), at least the first of these limits is dropped: One's property rights are violated if some object over which one has established title through the conventionally established procedure is removed, whether or not the loss of that object affects one at all.[4] Thus, the conventions establishing forms of appropriation, if legitimate, extend a person's rights to the forebearance of others beyond what the primitive right to noninterference establishes. And these extended rights stand in need of justification, particularly since the main interest people have in acquiring title to goods that are not of direct use in satisfying those needs protected by the primitive right of noninterference lies in the power those goods bring to command the services of others.

Thus, a system of property is a nonvoluntary social institution in a strong sense. The problem of explaining how a system of rights and prerogatives can be morally binding on people even without their actual consent has most often been confronted as the problem of political obligation; but the interest of Hume's analysis, presented above, lies just in the observation that the state is only one among many institutions presenting this same difficulty. One approach to this problem that is familiar from discussions of the political case is the notion of hypothetical agreement. Suppose we could establish that, if the participants in a given institution were in a position freely to decide whether or not to cooperate on the terms that institution provides, then it would be rational for them to agree to these terms. This might be taken to provide some reason for believing that institution to be legitimate and for regarding complaints against its requirements as unjustified. Suppose, on the other hand, it were conceded that some of the persons to whom a given institution applies would have no reason to accept cooperation on the terms it offers them if they had a chance to choose. In that case, we would have to admit that the institution was not wholly legitimate and that it rested to some degree on mere coercion or on some members' taking advantage of the inability of others to refuse to participate.[5] Such an argument, by appeal to hypothetical agreement, is inescapably contrary to fact, it relies on claims about what would be the case if some admittedly false assumption were to hold. But the argument is not essentially concerned with an imaginary convocation of fictional persons. The question at issue remains, what do present persons regard as reasonable terms of cooperation? The function of the notion of a hypothetical contract is merely to serve as a framework within which arguments about what terms are reasonable can be set forth in a general way. It is useful to the degree to which it leads arguments about terms of cooperation to be formulated in helpful and enlightening ways.

THE HYPOTHETICAL CONTRACT MODEL

The idea of possible unanimous agreement on terms of cooperation as even a necessary condition for the legitimacy of social institutions already embodies a certain moral point of view, a kind of formal egalitarianism. This moral standpoint is not wholly uncontroversial, but it need not be taken as a matter of controversy in our consideration of market institutions, since most of the relevant arguments for or against markets, e.g., those intuitive arguments for markets considered at the outset of this chapter, are ones which could be offered within a hypothetical contract framework. The moral content of the idea of hypothetical agreement is increased as we move beyond mere formal egalitarianism—beyond the idea that institutions must be justified to each of their members—to include particular judgments as to what considerations should or should not be recognized as legitimate grounds on which members may refuse to accept given terms of cooperation. In forms of hypothetical contract argument that rely heavily upon the device of a hypothetical contractual situation, judgments about the relevant grounds for accepting or rejecting such principles may be built in, in the form of restrictions on the knowledge and motivation of the parties to the contract.[6] Thus, for example, the parties, assumed to be self-interested, may be assumed not to know what talents or disabilities they may have, the idea being that they are thereby deprived of any grounds for favoritism towards the able or the disabled. As we will see later, however, once such "improper" influences are screened out it may still not be clear how the proper weighting of various conflicting interests is to be determined. Further, such restrictions on knowledge require justification, and it seems that an adequate justification would have to address directly the moral points at issue, namely why it is that some claims are morally relevant and others are not and why some morally relevant claims take precedence over others.

There is a dilemma here for the advocate of the hypothetical contract model. If one sticks closely to the position I have called *formal egalitarianism*, then the model appears quite weak. On the other hand, as more content is built into the model, and the conditions under which hypothetical agreement is reached become more and more different from the point of view of actual citizens, the model itself becomes increasingly difficult to justify, and whatever controversy surrounds the particular conclusions reached is transferred to the controversial features of the model. In what follows I will stay closer to the former alternative, trying to show how the weaker form of the hypothetical contract model can be used to deal with one argument in favor of markets. This will mean that problems of balancing competing interests must be faced as independent moral issues rather than brought within the contract framework in the form of assumptions about the knowledge or motivation of the contracting parties. The result may be, however, that the hypothetical contract is left with a severely diminished role.

Our concern, then, is with those basic institutions of a society that apply to all of its members without their consent. Very roughly, the benefits and burdens associated with these institutions can be thought of as falling into the following broad categories: On the side of benefits, the basic institutions of a society will, first, define the personal and property rights of individual members, their rights to the forebearance of others, and their powers to alter their relationship to others through voluntary undertakings. Second, these institutions may provide for the enforcement of these rights by creating positions of special authority and responsibility, e.g., the police, the judicial system, etc. Finally, institutions may create agencies to provide other goods and services, including both public goods and distributable goods such as health care, guaranteed income, etc., and may specify what rights individual members have to claim shares in these goods. Obviously, none of these goods can be provided without corresponding contributions. The legitimacy of institutions, in the sense in which we have been discussing it, is just their moral title to require such contributions without prior consent (i.e., to require of those to whom the institutions apply that they refrain from invasion of the personal and property rights which those institutions specify, that they acknowledge and not interfere with the authority assigned to its officials, and that they contribute in those ways required by the institutions to the maintenance of the system of enforcement and to the provision of whatever other benefits the institutions provide.)

MARKETS, OBLIGATIONS, AND LIBERTY

Proponents of market institutions typically advocate that the nonvoluntarily incurred obligations of members of society be kept to a minimum by keeping to a minimum those benefits guaranteed to all members simply *qua* members. Of course market proponents divide over just where the appropriate minimum of benefits lies—whether, for example, roads or schools should be provided for all via compulsory taxation or left to individual initiative. But, without getting into the details of these particular controversies, we can consider in general some arguments raised in favor of leaving a larger sphere to the operation of the market. Some of these arguments appeal to considerations of efficiency, to the alleged efficiency of market mechanisms as means of allocating factors of production or as methods for distributing the social product. I will touch briefly on distributive considerations, but I will focus my main attention on a different and, I think, more fundamental argument. This is the claim that considerations of liberty require the minimization of nonvoluntarily incurred obligations and, correspondingly, the maximization of the sphere left to truly voluntary arrangements, i.e., to the market. This claim is the natural successor to the argument, considered earlier, that took free contract as the basis of all legitimate social obligations, once that argument is trimmed back in recognition of the fact that the basic institutions of society are bound to involve some nonvoluntary component.[7]

To properly appraise this argument it is important to

distinguish various bases on which one may object to the obligations imposed by given social institutions. I will argue that the force of many arguments in favor of market institutions, in particular that of some arguments recently offered by Robert Nozick (1973, 1974), depends on a failure to distinguish different forms of political and economic unliberty. Once these are distinguished one can, if one wishes, accept in quite a strong form the libertarian intuitions to which these arguments appeal without being forced to accept their conclusions. A subsidiary effect of the following discussion is to point up the degree to which we stand in need of a set of categories of economic liberty adequate to modern conditions. Political liberty is commonly conceived (both in the philosophical tradition and in public discussion) in terms of a highly developed set of categories: freedom of speech and of the press, specific forms of political participation and representation, etc. One can debate the degree to which these notions are adequate to conditions in the modern state, but at least they provide us with starting points for discussion that have a firm place in the public mind and have been thoroughly explored and carefully articulated over a long period of time. But neither the tradition of political philosophy nor common understanding provides us with a comparable set of categories of economic liberty. Perhaps the notions of property rights and freedom of contract constitute a set of categories that once played this role, but as I shall argue below these do not constitute an adequate conception of economic liberty. To move beyond laissez faire we need to develop such a conception, but at present none has established itself either in the public mind or in political philosophy. Arguments in this area frequently rely on familiar notions imported from politics and law such as due process, representation, etc. These are no doubt relevant, but they need to be justified and perhaps circumscribed by being placed within a more general theory of liberty in the economic sphere.

I am not going to present or even sketch a theory of economic liberty here. I will merely consider three different ways in which the obligations imposed by various social institutions can be compared and criticized. These are:

1. To what extent are the citizens of an institution legally free to avoid the obligations it imposes by renouncing their citizenship altogether?

2. How deeply do the obligations imposed by an institution interfere with the ability of members to exercise control over their lives and activities?
3. To what extent are present citizens able (e.g., through political mechanisms) to control the form that their obligations take?

I will comment briefly on each of these in turn.

Renunciation of Citizenship

Certainly one way in which institutions can fail to meet the requirements of moral legitimacy is by being overly restrictive of the right of citizens to opt out. The extent of this right is a question that has been insufficiently explored in the literature of political philosophy. I do not know what a complete account of this matter would look like, but a few points seem reasonably clear. Presumably, a state could legitimately restrict exit when this was necessary to enforce private contracts. To this end, if circumstances required it, perhaps a state could enforce a short waiting period after one's announced intention to leave, in order to give possible creditors an opportunity to state their claims. It also seems plausible that some social benefits, such as special forms of training, could legitimately carry requirements of service that would have to be fulfilled before exit would be permitted. (If this is true, it is uncontroversially so only where the goods in question figure in the lives of members of the society in such a way that their acceptance can be regarded as truly voluntary. Some forms of education may meet this requirement, but others will not.) A more controversial question is whether in some emergency situations a government could legitimately restrict exit in order to retain enough able citizens to meet a present threat. Is some explicit "fair warning" required before such a restriction on exit can be enforced? If not, then the legitimacy of the restriction seems to involve appeal to the idea that remaining in the society in general involves a voluntary acceptance of the risk of being unable to leave should an emergency arise. These unsystematic observations suggest to me that the right of exit can legitimately be restricted only as a result of a voluntary undertaking whose consequences are publicly known. For citizens who have made no such undertakings this right is virtually absolute.

Imposition of Obligations

Contributions required of members as a condition for their continued receipt of benefits may vary in the degree to which they intrude into the members' lives and interfere with their control over their activities and over the development and exercise of their talents. For example, the contribution required of members may be more or less specific in the form of activity it requires. One reason why taxation seems generally thought to be a more acceptable form of required contribution than, say, a system of required tasks or a requirement of payments in kind is that it leaves citizens with greater latitude in deciding how to arrange their lives while still meeting their social obligations.[8] Of course the enforcement of such required contributions is only one of the ways in which institutions may restrict or enhance the ability of their members to exercise effective control over their productive lives (and over how much of their lives are devoted to production). If we are appraising institutions on this score we should therefore be concerned not merely with this one obligation but rather with the total effect that a set of institutions has on the de facto ability of its members to exercise this kind of effective self-regulation.

To give a systematic account of when some institutions are to be preferred to others on this basis, or even an analysis of the various dimensions along which comparisons of this kind should be carried out, would require at least the beginnings of a theory of this particular form of liberty. I have no such theory. It seems likely that the relative importance generally attached to avoiding various forms of intrusion and to maintaining particular forms of control may be quite different in different societies (and the forms of control and intrusion with which people are concerned will vary too). Searching for a single general principle in this area, perhaps one might try a modified version of Rawls' (1971, sec. 82) claim about the priority of political liberty: Once the level of material well-being in a society reaches a point at which the most urgent needs are met and the development of one's capacities and pursuit of one's special interests for their own sake becomes a possibility, people will have an increasing marginal preference for effective control over their own productive activities relative to competing considerations of economic efficiency. The claim that such a preference would be rational is a least no less plausible in the economic case than in the political case where Rawls employed it. Moreover, such a general preference seems at first to be more promising as a theoretical basis for economic than for political liberty. But this contrast now seems doubtful. Rawls' appeal to increasing marginal preference, taken as a complete theory of political liberty, would be unsatisfying, quite apart from any doubts about the reality of this preference, because it leaves the object of the preference—the liberties themselves—unaccounted for. A list of such liberties is more or less taken as given. But a large part of what one wants from a philosophical account of political liberty is an explanation of what liberties are or should be included on the list, what structure they have, and why. In the economic case we bring with us no such list of liberties to be explained and analyzed, hence this dissatisfaction does not come immediately to mind. But dissatisfaction reemerges once we ask what the preference asserted is a preference *for*. Certainly it is not simply a preference for, say, more leisure time over a greater output of material goods (or vice versa), or one for a redefinition of tasks in order to make jobs more varied and less tedious even if longer hours are then required to produce the same goods. Rather, it is a preference for mechanisms that enable one to affect such choices.

Citizens' Control of Obligations

This brings us to the third question mentioned above, namely the extent to which the current citizens of a given institution are able, through political processes or otherwise, to control and modify the form that their institutional obligations take. Even if the requirements that citizenship imposes on us at any given time are to a large extent inherited from previous generations, the degree to which we (or a majority of us) are empowered to modify them if we so choose is an important factor in their acceptability. Political power that, even under ideal conditions, can be controlled by a mere majority, does not have the legitimizing force of consent. It does make some difference, however, as is shown in the widespread feeling that there is a special objection to the conscription of citizens who have not yet reached voting age.

To turn now to the particular question at issue, suppose that we are considering a set of institutions that constitute a full-blown welfare state, guaranteeing education, health care, and an assured minimum standard of living to all its citizens. These benefits can be offered only on the basis of some regular contributions, part of which, we may suppose, take the form of a tax system that diminishes the rate at which citizens can benefit from voluntary commercial arrangements with one another. Suppose that there will be some members of such a society whose income is less than what they could command if they could bargain with their fellow citizens on an unregulated market, holding out for the maximum others would be willing to pay to secure their services. If some of these members are able, from a practical point of view, to exercise their right to opt out, then they may have a choice between remaining members on the terms now offered them or bargaining with the society from without as free agents and, thereby, let us suppose, obtaining a higher income.

This possibility may be seen as posing a practical problem for nonmarket institutions, namely the problem that they may be unstable, or at least inefficient, because they are continually subject to the defection of their most talented and valuable members.[9] But the problem also has a theoretical form, which is of greater interest for our present purposes. Whether or not anyone ever overcomes his own inertia and becomes a "free agent" (or is bargained away by a competing society), the fact, if it were a fact, that it would always be rational for those members of a cooperative system who have economically valuable talents to drop out of the system, and irrational for them to stay, would raise a question about even the theoretical viability of that system. Here one may argue that this objection rests on an artifically narrow view of the relevant grounds of rational preference. Membership in a cooperative association of equals, in which the needs of all are provided for and in which each is motivated to contribute by his perception of the needs of the group and his obligations to it, may itself be counted an important and valuable good. When this good, and other particular values for which this kind of association may be a precondition, are taken into account, it is by no means obvious that even rigorously egalitarian nonmarket institutions will be subject to the theoretical charge of irrationality in a damaging form, provided that such institutions are able to provide their members with the material requirements of a decent life.

But reasonable people may differ over the value to be attached to such goods of community and over the exact price it is rational to pay for their enjoyment. This poses a problem for our application of the hypothetical contract model. Despite the fact that there are plausible, or even very generally shared, ends and values relative to which participation in given institutions is a rational choice, there may be some people who find themselves living under these institutions for whom such participation is not worth its costs, given the ends and values they actually hold. For such people, the fact that their institutions are the object of *possible* hypothetical consent on the basis of other postulated goals may be small comfort. Where opting out is a practical as well as a legal possibility, this problem does not seem pressing; these people can always emigrate. But what of those for whom emigration may not be a practical alternative?

Internal Emigration

As long as there are some people in this position of would-be emigrants the contractualists' claim that it would be rational for everyone, given a free choice, to consent to the prevailing institutions is literally false: There are some members whose cooperation rests, finally, on their inability to leave. This theoretical difficulty could be eased, and the would-be emigrants given as much as they could ask for, if they were given the chance to opt out legally, without leaving home physically; i.e., to transfer directly to a special status of resident aliency with rights and duties they might obtain by emigrating, and to deal with their former compatriots as foreigners.[10] Indeed, one could argue that if the right to opt out is as absolute as suggested above then it requires us to recognize such a right of "internal emigration." Essentially this claim is advanced by Nozick (1973, p. 70; 1974, pp. 173-174). Acceptance of this argument might well aggravate the practical instability mentioned earlier. More interesting, however, is its apparent theoretical effect of turning all legitimate institutions into ones that approximate a system of free contract of the type favored by market advocates. Through the institutions of a welfare state the members of a society can offer one another whatever terms of cooperation they choose but, if this argument is accepted, members would have to be free to take those terms or to reject them if they felt they could do better for themselves by bargaining with their fellows as social emigrés-at-home.

But must this argument be accepted? I think not. The distinction between free external emigration and free internal emigration has an importance that goes beyond the practical differences between these two forms of exiting. In both cases it is important to ask what is the source of the system of contract relations and property rights under which the free agents deal with their former associates and legally own what they gain as a result of these transactions? In examples of external emigration, what is usually appealed to is some supposed "natural" system of contract and property rights. In practice, of course, an emigré would have to go somewhere; presumably, therefore, he would be bound by the specific institutions of contract and property prevailing in his new society (and with respect to these, the questions of legitimacy with which we began could be raised anew). But the examples as they are usually presented seem to presuppose a kind of Howard Hughes or Robert Vesco who is always able to find a haven from which he can deal with the rest of us on whatever terms he can get us to accept. What we have in such examples is thus not a fixed system of property and exchange, but some *ad hoc* extrainstitutional arrangement.

The case of internal emigration, however, presents quite a different situation. As long as the emigrés remain at home, there profits, if truly *theirs*, must be so under the system of property rights enforced by the prevailing institutions of their (old) society. So the argument for the right of internal emigration, if it is successful, does not merely require that the nonmarket society enter into *ad hoc* bargains with external "pirates," but also that it become a market society itself, enforcing contracts with the emigrés and enforcing their rights to keep what they gain through these transactions. To do this involves not only releasing some people from their obligations but at the same time enforcing a system of rights that gives the would-be emigrés new economic power over their fellow citizens. A justification of such a move must, therefore, involve justification of this power; it will have to involve consideration of, on the one hand, the claims of the emigrés—not claims to be allowed to leave, but to create new terms of cooperation—and, on the other hand, the claims of the other citizens—not claims to command the services of the emigrés, but claims to be free from, e.g., the kind of domination that results from great concentration of wealth in a few hands. By contrast, in considering a genuine right to leave, we would be concerned with, on the one hand, the liberty of the emigrés to free themselves altogether of unwanted institutional ties and, on the other, whatever claims on their services other members of society may have. As I have suggested above, it seems likely that this question is relatively easy to resolve.

Thus a right of internal emigration of the sort that would turn all legitimate institutions into market institutions cannot be derived from the right to opt out (even if this right is virtually absolute). The case for internal emigration would have to be made on the basis of arguments about the forms of control that those who are and remain citizens should be allowed to exercise over their own contributions and those of others.

CONCLUSIONS

This brings me to parts (2) and (3) of my analysis of the obligation to contribute. Enforcement, either of a pure system of free contract or of a system of highly qualified property rights, will involve restricting some alternatives that might otherwise be open to people. Can we say that a system of free contract is clearly preferable to a nonmarket system on the ground that the restrictions involved intrude less on citizens' control over the development and exercise of their talents? I do not see that this is so.

I begin with a purely negative philosophical point, which I hope is clear from what has gone before. From the fact that institutions of a certain form involve a minimum of nonvoluntary obligations it does not follow that such institutions are to be preferred to others on the grounds that they best promote the relevant forms of liberty. To settle this issue of liberty one must take up the complex empirical question of what the consequences will be, under given social and economic conditions, of the adoption of various institutional arrangements. In particular, it must be shown what the consequences are for the ability of various individuals in the society to maintain control over their own lives and pursuits.

Under a range of possible and, in our experience, not uncommon circumstances, establishment of a system of property rights based on free contract means that some people, in order to gain the means to life, have to devote virtually all their productive energies to whatever tasks and pursuits are desired by those who control the goods necessary for life in their society. The claim of nonmarket institutions is that they can prevent this kind of domination through restrictions on distribution and ownership. Doing this may involve placing limits on how much people can come to own and will also involve decreasing, through taxation, the rate at which people can benefit from the scarcity of their particular talents. It may also involve requiring a certain minimum contribution from every able member of the society as a condition for continued rights to social benefits.[11] Even institutions involving obligations of this sort need not involve direct restrictions on citizens' choice of occupations. Nor is it immediately apparent that such a system would represent a diminution rather than an enlargement of people's ability to choose forms of productive activity that they find rewarding. Certainly, there is much to be learned about the difficult empirical question of how such control can be preserved and enhanced within large scale economic institutions. I cannot here defend a claim about what the best answer to this question is in any particular case or about the role that restricted market mechanisms might play in such an answer. Instead, I will offer in closing one further philosophical remark about the form that the argument for such an answer should take.

The argument presented here suggests that in choosing between nonmarket institutions and market institutions we face a choice between institutions that restrict the liberty of some people—those who would do well to become "emigrés" or those for whom the values of community rank relatively low—and institutions that restrict the liberty of others—those who would be subject to the control of others in a market society or those who set a high value on the goods of community. There is no way to frame institutions so as to satisfy both of these groups. Thus, assuming that each generation will include some representatives of each group, no matter how we frame our institutions, some people will be faced, without their consent, with institutions that, in most obvious sense, they would not have chosen.

As mentioned earlier, one way to deal with this difficulty within the hypothetical contract framework is to say that institutions are legitimate if they are in accord with principles which parties would choose if forced to make their choice without knowing which of the two groups they belonged to. I want to suggest here another way of understanding the argument. This approach may reach the same conclusions as the "veil of ignorance" method, but it may avoid at least some of its apparent problems.

Suppose we face the fact that there is no way to resolve our conflict that will be literally acceptable to both sides. Nevertheless, we will try to preserve the idea that we must be able to *justify* our choice to all of the parties concerned. If the choice goes against the potential emigrés, we can say to them: We realize that this system denies your opportunities you would like to have, but adopting a system that involved the general enforcement of the rights you seek would mean asking some people to accept a system that made them, to a very high degree, subservient to your wishes. On the other hand, if the choice goes in favor of the potential emigrés and against the remaining residents, we can say to them: We are sorry, but we could not do better for you without asking others to accept limits on the degree to which they can benefit from the scarcity of their talents, an upper limit on wealth, and the possibility of a required minimum contribution to society.

Of course, the exact form of these responses will depend on prevailing circumstances and the nature and consequences of the institutions they require. But in general, in the kind of circumstances we are most familiar with, it seems to me that the second response is in a clear sense going to be the weaker one. If this is so, then it provides us with a kind of contractualist argument in favor of nonmarket institutions—a ground for claiming that such institutions are justifiable to all concerned, in a way that pure market institutions are not.

A few remarks about this argument are in order. First, it involves a kind of balancing of interests; it appeals to our intuitive judgment that what one group stands to lose is weightier than what the other stands to gain. What kind of weighing is going on here?[12] One interpretation of the hypothetical contract argument suggests that it is a comparison of the strength of individual preferences. What is claimed is that individuals on both sides of the controversy must admit that *they* set a higher value on avoiding certain intrusions into their lives than on avoiding others. But would we modify our conclusion if the parties on one side of the dispute had genuinely different preferences (e.g., if they cared about nothing so much as keeping open the chance to strike it really rich)? If we would not, then what is appealed to in our argument is not mere preference but a judgment with moral content that requires explanation and defense. Even if it is individual preferences that are being balanced, however, the argument is not a utilitarian one. This is shown by the fact that it involves no appeal to the relative sizes of the two groups. If a genuine summing of interests were involved, these numbers would be crucial.

There are several ways in which my conclusion could be avoided. One would be to maintain that the forms of acquisition that the would-be emigrés wish their institutions to recognize are part of a natural right of property; therefore, the decision against the emigrés does not merely deny the fulfillment of an interest (as a decision against the other members of the society would), but also infringes on a right.[13] I have argued briefly against this position. Another way to deny my conclusion would be to maintain that, as a matter of distributive justice, there is a specific level of return to which the holders of scarce talents are entitled and that nonmarket institutions are unjust insofar as they interfere with these just returns. This does not strike me as a plausible line for a defender of market institutions to take. Given the degree to which the distributions effected by markets are dependent on chance considerations involving the distribution of talents and the pattern of tastes in a society, it seems unlikely that there is any plausible distributive pattern to which the outcome of market institutions will generally conform. But I have not dealt with such distributive considerations here. My argument has been, rather, that insofar as one moves away from particular distributive criteria and focuses instead on considerations of liberty, the case for pure market institutions does not appear to be as strong as is sometimes supposed.

ACKNOWLEDGMENTS

Since the Battelle Conference I have had the opportunity to read later versions of this paper for a number of audiences to whom I am indebted for many comments and suggestions. I am also grateful to Charles Beitz, G. A. Cohen, Adam Morton, and William Talbott for written comments which have helped me to improve the paper.

NOTES

1. As given in Hume, 1739, Book III, Part II, Sec. V.

2. In an earlier version of this paper I was myself inclined to overlook it and to contrast institutions of promising and institutions of property more sharply in this regard. For clarification on this point I am indebted to G. A. Cohen.

3. Compare these with the two restrictions on the acquisition of property in the state of nature set forth by Locke (1690, Ch. V) viz., first, that the goods actually be used and not wasted by the possessor, and, second, that there be "enough and as good" left for others. Locke himself distinguishes (Sec. 50) between the primitive notion of property so restricted and systems of property founded on consent in which these restrictions are relaxed.

4. As is shown by the fact that those who deny that any right is violated in such cases commonly describe themselves as rejecting property. Godwin (1798, Bk. VIII), for example, so describes his doctrine that a person has no right to an object if that person's possession of it produces less utility than its possession by someone else to whom it could be transferred. But he sees his further doctrine that people have a right not to have their possessions forcibly removed (even when they have no right to retain them) as constituting a reintroduction of property rights. It is, of course, not obvious that these two doctrines can be made consistent.

5. This statement of the intuitive basis of the appeal to a hypothetical contract is close to that given by John Rawls (see, e.g., Rawls, 1969, especially pp. 144-145). The idea of *possible* unanimous agreement as a necessary condition for the legitimacy of coercive institutions was clearly stated by Kant (1797, Sec. 47).

6. This is the form of Rawls' theory, as presented in Rawls (1971, especially sec. 24).

7. Milton Friedman (1974) emphasizes the primacy of liberty in the case for market institutions. Considerations of liberty are also central to Robert Nozick's (1973, 1974) antiredistributive arguments.

8. Nozick (1973, pp. 65-66; 1974, p. 169) makes light of the attempt to distinguish between taxation and forced labor on this basis, pointing out that there is a "gradation of systems of forced labor, from one that specifies a particular activity, to one that gives a choice among two activities, to . . . ; and so on up." But this does not seem to me to show that some systems in this series are not morally preferable to others.

9. For an interesting discussion of an actual instance of this problem, see Bernstein (1974). The question at issue is how worker-owned firms, orgainized on the basis of equal distribution of profits, cope with the fact that certain specialty jobs generally command a wage higher than the equal monthly advance against profits that cooperative firms can offer. The answer is, generally, by hiring these specialists as outside "free agents" rather than sacrificing the principle of equal sharing among members. The example is particularly appropriate for the promarket argument considered here, since the firms are operating within a larger market economy that provides a framework within which the free agents can deal with the firms.

10. "*A* status of resident alien" rather than "the status," since I am here supposing that the emigrés are granted the economic status of free agents, and resident aliens are not generally accorded such privileges. For a philosophical discussion of the status of resident aliens in historical societies, and an argument for the recognition of such status as a refuge from some obligations to contribute (particularly from conscription), see Walzer (1970, Ch. 5).

11. "As a condition," since I think institutions might well allow people to opt out of the economic system without leaving the country if they wished to be genuine nonparticipants in the economy. Such persons would not raise the difficulties presented by resident free agents since they would not exercise economic power over other members of the society.

12. The problem raised in the next few sentences is discussed more fully in Scanlon (1975).

13. This is an important part of Nozick's argument as I understand it.

REFERENCES

Berstein, P. (1974) "Run Your Own Business: Worker-owned Plywood Firms," *Working Papers for a New Society*, 2(2), 24-34.

Friedman, M. (with J. Vaizey) (1974) "Equality and Income," *The Listener* 91, May, pp. 688-690.

Godwin, W. (1798) *Enquiry Concerning Political Justice* (3rd. ed.). (K. C. Carter, ed., Abridged ed. Oxford: Oxford University Press, 1971.)

Hume, D. (1752) *"Of the Original Contract."* (In C. W. Hendel, ed., *David Hume's Political Essays.* New York: Liberal Arts, 1953, pp. 43–61.)

Hume, D. (1739) *A Treatise of Human Nature.* (In L. A. Selby-Bigge, ed., Oxford: Oxford University Press, 1888.)

Kant, I. (1797) *The Metaphysics of Morals,* Part II. (Transl. by J. Ladd as *Metaphysical Elements of Justice.* Indianapolis: Bobbs-Merrill, 1965.)

Locke, J. (1690) *Second Treatise of Government.* (In T. P. Peardon, ed., New York: Liberal Arts, 1952.)

Nozick, R. (1973) "Distributive Justice," *Philosophy and Public Affairs,* 3, 45–126.

Nozick, R. (1974) *Anarchy, State and Utopia.* New York: Basic.

Rawls, J. (1969) "Justice as Fairness." In P. Laslett and W. G. Runciman, eds., *Philosophy, Politics and Society* (2nd series). Oxford: Basil Blackwell, pp. 132–157.

Rawls, J. (1971) *A Theory of Justice.* Cambridge, Mass.: Harvard University Press.

Scanlon, T. (1975) "Preference and Urgency," *Journal of Philosophy,* 72, pp. 655–670.

Singer, P. (1973) "Altruism and Commerce: A Defense of Titmuss against Arrow," *Philosophy and Public Affairs* 2, 312–323.

Singer, P. (1977) "Freedoms and Utilities in the Distribution of Health Care." Chapter 9, this volume.

Walzer, M. (1970) *Obligations: Essays on Disobedience, War, and Citizenship.* Cambridge, Mass.: Harvard University Press.

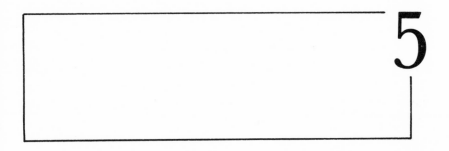

POLITICAL EQUALITY AND PRIVATE PROPERTY: THE DISTRIBUTIONAL PARADOX

JAMES M. BUCHANAN
Virginia Polytechnic Institute and State University

INTRODUCTION

In this chapter I shall advance an explanatory hypothesis concerning widely held attitudes toward the distributive outcomes produced in an economy that is organized largely on market or exchange principles. I shall argue that these attitudes stem from an emergent contradiction within modern liberal individualism, a contradiction that can be neither readily resolved nor easily ignored. Public property rights, embodied in the voting franchise, have come into being through modern political institutions, in both their idealized and operative forms. We seek to use these rights to modify the distribution or assignment of private property among persons and families to conform with vague ideals of equality, while at the same time we try to limit the encroachment of the State on spheres of private action.

Political equality among persons, defined in terms of the voting franchise, is basically inconsistent with continuing economic differences. The individual's right to vote, held on an equal basis with other people, implies an ultimate equality in a political claim to all wealth in society. Observed economic inequalities among persons must therefore be subject to predicted political intrusion. But this political thrust toward the elimination of economic differences, toward economic equality, is at the same time inconsistent with individual freedom from the State. "Political equality to use power within appropriately defined limits" may be reconciled with "the legal protection of private property within appropriately defined limits," but the delicate balance that is required to accomplish this reconciliation may be overreached. The attempt to allow the full exercising of public property rights held equally by all participants in democratic order may produce ill-conceived interventions in market adjustment to the disadvantage of everyone.

Many of those who criticize the distributive results of a market economy draw the wrong implications about causal elements and hence seem largely to misdirect their emphases. They should not, basically, be concerned about the distribution of the potentially realizable surplus that market exchanges bring into being—the only distribution that is, strictly speaking, attributable to the market process. The institution generating the distribution of these gains from trade is a misconceived target.[1] What these critics are concerned about is, instead, the pretrade or premarket distribution of endowments, talents, and capacities (of *wealth* defined to include human as well as nonhuman capital), which is a much more important element in determining the observed posttrade distribution than the market itself. To make the market, as a social organization, responsible for the imputation of premarket positions confuses the issue, especially in terms of implications for social and political policy. The market takes persons as they are, differences and all, and allows *mutual* gains to be secured. Distributional attention should be focused on pretrade or premarket positions of persons and families, with the recognition that, under any conceivable distribution, whether this be "natural," historically determined, or arbitrarily imposed, the market process itself insures mutuality of gain.

There may be differentials in bargaining power and in bargaining skills that modify the distribution of the net gains from trade within narrow limits. But broadly speaking, the potentially realizable surplus that trade makes possible is shared among all traders, and certainly no trader finds himself made worse off in absolute terms in his posttrade position than in his pretrade position. However, what we observe is postmarket distribution. With no knowledge of premarket disposition of endowments, we are tempted to impute to the exchange process itself causal influence that it simply does not possess. This may, in turn, lead to mistaken and misapplied prohibitions and limitations on the exchange process which may damage all parties, with little or no effects on the distribution of relative endowments and talents.

EQUAL ENDOWMENTS

It is helpful to break down the separate causal influences that may generate realized differences among persons in command over final product values. Consider first a model in which all persons possess identical endowments and capacities but in which individual preferences differ;[2] that is to say, all persons enter the market process on an equal basis. Because of differences among utility functions, however, the postmarket distribution of final product values will be unequal. Even in a no-production economy, those persons whose preferences embody somewhat more flexibility among final product items will, on observation, seem to fare better than those whose tastes dictate relatively high evaluations for specific commodities. For the latter, market exchange may involve large sacrifices in initial endowments, in a physically measured sense, in order to attain relatively limited increments in the amounts of those items that are intensely desired. For example, the person in Greenland who has an abiding passion for fresh coconuts will seem demonstrably worse off than a neighbor for whom fish are equally delectable.

If we introduce production from human effort, the market organization of the identical-endowments model will also tend to generate differences in final product allocation that reflect attitudes toward risk. In any single period of observation, some of those persons who are not averse to risk will have "struck it rich" in comparison with those in the community who shun risk. Some gamblers are always rich.

Most important, perhaps, are those persons who place a relatively low value on leisure who will secure a relatively large share of measured end values of produced commodities. There may appear to be substantial differences among persons and families in "real income" in such a market economy because the value of leisure is not normally incorporated in such measures. Finally, chance itself may enter; a "little bit of luck" may create private fortunes, even in the world where endowments and capacities are identical among all persons.[3]

In any of the settings just discussed, there will emerge apparent asymmetries in the postmarket distribution of final consumables. There is, however, no legitimate basis for prohibiting or restricting market exchange in any commodity or service so long as individual preferences are accepted as controlling and so long as consumption externalities are absent. The call girl sells her services because she values them less than that which she can secure in exchange; she does so not because of some relative deprivation in economic endowment, but because this behavior is dictated by her intrinsic pattern of preferences. The same thing applies to the wino who indirectly trades his blood for alcohol.

This identical-endowments model becomes the idealized setting for laissez-faire precepts. In the premarket assignment of endowments and capacities, all persons are economic equals. Observed differences in command over final product value stem exclusively from choice or chance, and there is no contradiction among the trading process, the market, and democratic political order, where each person is assigned an equal share in ultimate political power. Limitations on the exchange process might emerge here, but these would reflect the presence of recognized externalities. There would be no grounds for proposing distributionally motivated interferences with the market process.

DIFFERENCES IN ENDOWMENTS WITH EQUAL PREFERENCES

Let us now shift to an alternative model that allows differences among persons in either initial endowments or in capacities to produce values or both. To clarify the discussion, let us now assume that all persons are identical in preferences; utility functions are the same for all individuals.

In this setting, let us say that one person, A, is observed to purchase personal services from another person, B. Both parties clearly gain from the transaction, and any overt restriction on the freely negotiated exchange would probably place both parties in less preferred positions. Individual A, the purchaser of personal services in the example, may be able to secure the services of the other person, B, however, solely because of A's superior initial economic endowment. The result is exemplified quite clearly in the BBC series "Upstairs and Downstairs," which has been shown on Public Broadcasting Corporation television programs in the United States. Those who lived "upstairs" in Edwardian England dominated the lives of those who lived "downstairs" (the domestic staff) despite the demonstrable personal superiority of some members of the downstairs group. Given the distribution of initial endowments, that is, the legally sanctioned structure of property rights (which in Edwardian England included rights of class position as well as rights to measurable assets), attempts to restrict market activity would probably have caused damage to all parties. Such attempts, however, have often been observed to take place because of the failure to distinguish carefully between the distribution of property rights and the trading of these rights. To continue with the Edwardian England example, attempts to improve the competitiveness of the market for domestic servants, to introduce potential mobility among prospective employers, might have reduced, and perhaps substantially, the subservience of the domestic servants as a group and individually. Strictly speaking, competitiveness in the structure of markets can eliminate the "master–servant" relationship in a personal sense. But market exchange between persons with vastly different economic endowments may still embody the performance of services by one person for another that would not take place in the absence of such differences. The exchange, as such, may be wholly voluntary, and there may be no economic exploitation in the process. Yet the willingness of one person to perform personal services for the other may stem, at base, from the first person's relatively sparse endowment rather than from any personal preference to pursue such an occupation.

Economists have not been especially helpful in sorting out the confusion here, even if they have recognized the issues. Their domain is that of exchange, or contract, and too often they have seemed content to relegate distributional issues to one side, to separate these all too sharply from allocative questions. But, of course, distribution is what matters in this context, the distribution of relative endowments, of rights, in pretrade or premarket positions. Only within the last two decades have economists commenced to look at property rights in any serious analytical fashion.

HOBBESIAN ANARCHY AND THE EMERGENCE OF PROPERTY RIGHTS

But what can economists say? I have recently written a book in which I try to examine the conceptual origins of individual rights from an initial situation of Hobbesian anarchy, the war of each against all (Buchanan, 1975). My ultimate purpose in this book is to see what, if anything, we can say about *changes* in an existing distribution of premarket endowments (rights) among separate members of a defined political community. Forcing ourselves to think of the setting for genuine Hobbesian anarchy is helpful, since it prompts the realization that individuals need not be natural equals in the sheer struggle for survival that such anarchy embodies. Individuals would differ in physical strength, in intelligence, in inherent morality. Nonetheless, even when these differences are fully recognized, a *contractual* basis for the emergence of mutually respected rights can be derived.[4] All persons can gain from the negotiation and enforcement of an effective disarmament agreement, as Hobbes recognized and elaborated in his discussion of the basic contract with the sovereign. The point is that all persons can secure continuing mutual gains from a legal structure that implies both a definition of the appropriate spheres of individual action and the enforcement of these spheres as defined. There would be, of course, a wide range of outcomes that would satisfy the requirements for mutual gain implicit in the very notion of contract. There is no uniquely determinate outcome of any contractual or trading process, regardless of the number of participants.[5] But the point of emphasis is that any outcome within this set dominates the anarchistic alternative for all members of the community. The structure of rights legally agreed on does, therefore, have a direct relationship to that distribution of consumables that might emerge under anarchy, the *natural distribution*.[6] Once a determinate assignment of rights has been settled, however, there seems to be no prospect for a contractual or an agreed-on rearrangement without some change in the underlying structural elements. Changes from one distribution to another, a distribution of endowments, of rights, within the dominant set become analogous to shifts among outcomes in *n*-person, zero-sum games. Losers must exist alongside winners, and potential losers will not agree to play in advance.

In a purely static and formal model, this might be the end of discussion. But history is not static, and our whole objective is to say something that will contain relevance, however remote, for an evaluation of the current structure that has emerged through historical process. Passage through time necessarily involves changes in the underlying structural parameters that might have provided the basis for any initial contractual agreement. The natural distribution of talents in Hobbesian anarchy, which influences the relative positions of persons in the agreed-on structure of rights, may shift, in a real or in an apparent sense, and this may potentially destroy or threaten to destroy the dominance of an existing claims structure. Recognition of this may prompt contractual renegotiation, with subsequent changes in the distribution of endowments. I have discussed the potentiality for such renegotiations in some detail elsewhere, and I shall not elaborate the analysis here (Buchanan, 1975).

THE STATE AS ENFORCER

In what follows, I want to examine another potential and perhaps more important variable, that which measures the limits of State action. Even in an idealized and abstract setting, it is difficult to conceive of a complete and unchanging definition or assignment of property rights among persons in a community.

Some grey areas where individual rights to do things seem to come into conflict must almost necessarily be present from the onset of any contractual agreement. And this area can surely be predicted to expand through time, as initial delineations prove inapplicable to unforeseen interactions. In this area of potential conflicts of rights, persons are plunged back into something analogous to Hobbesian anarchy; at the edges, predictable order disappears.[7] Indeed, one conceptual measure of civil order lies in the relationship between that set of behavioral interactions that is regulated within well-defined and mutually respected rights and that set which involves interpersonal and intergroup conflicts. Any assignment of rights must, of course, be enforced, and a contract of government may bring into being the enforcer, which we may call the *Protective State*.[8] It is, therefore, a natural consequence that this agency, which is appropriately assigned a limited enforcer role, should also be granted powers of adjudicating conflicts among persons and private groups where claims come into dispute.

Conceptually, the rights of the created agency, the Protective State, are also defined in the initial contract of government in a constitution. As this agency assumes powers to adjudicate claims, however, it necessarily takes on a dominating role. There exists no agency above it to limit its own claims, to protect the rights of persons and groups against encroachment by the enforcing agency itself. This inherent paradox of government has, of course, been fully recognized since classical antiquity, but neither historical experience nor philosophical precept has done much toward resolution. To Hobbes, the paradox points necessarily toward the surrender of all rights to the sovereign, a hypothesis that history neither fully corroborates nor fully refutes. To many political philosophers, "limited government" is possible, and experience suggests that this possibility may sometimes be realized.

It is not my intent or purpose here, even if I were fully competent to do so, to discuss the instrumental means and devices through which the activities of government may be limited, through which private property may be made inviolate against claims made upon it by the sovereign. Historically and factually, there have been societies that succeeded in limiting the arbitrary action of those persons who make decisions in the name of the State. Constitutional limits have sometimes been descriptively meaningful, up to a point, despite the frequently observed gradual enhancement of State powers.

In the American setting, the stricture that private property may not be taken without "due process of law" has carried a degree of protection against overtly discriminatory behavior on the part of governments and their officials. This clause of the Constitution has been helpful in allowing individuals and private groups to carry on their ordinary market dealings in an atmosphere of stability and predictability that would not have been present in a setting where rights were subjected to continuous redefinition by governmental agency. Strictly interpreted, however, the due process clause, or its equivalent, would or could allow little or no scope for the exercise of individual rights to political equality. Private property rights, as historically determined, are perhaps far removed from any initial contract or from that natural distribution that might have emerged from some period of acquisition and struggle. But these rights, as existing, would be protected against encroachment, not only from private persons but also from government itself. In a regime of such strict constitutional interpretation, there could be little or no role for the instrumental use of the political process to secure modifications in distributional outcomes. Individuals might be "political equals" in some effective sense, but the allowable scope for political–governmental action would be so circumscribed as to make franchise impotent with respect to the achievement of distributional objectives.[9]

THE EXERCISE OF "PUBLIC PROPERTY RIGHTS"

The historical experience of the United States has embodied increasing demands that distributional outcomes be modified in the direction of greater equality, and an increasing acceptance of the view that positive governmental action toward this end is fully appropriate, representing individuals' exercise of their claimed rights to political equality. Empirically, these demands have seemed too strong to be resisted by a fragile legalism that offered apparent protection to an arbitrary and historically determined pattern of individuals' claims to assets—a pattern that has seemed to many to possess little consensual foundations. Predictably, governments have responded to these demands, and by necessity this has implied increasing restriction on the exercise of legally santioned rights to the use of private property, broadly interpreted. "Political equality," expressed indirectly through the ballot box, came to dominate "private property" protected by the existing legal assignment of claims.

Nonetheless, both the legislative arm of government, which most directly gives expression to the demands of constituents, and the judicial arm, which embodies the enforcement of the legal order, recognized, at least implicitly, the dangers of allowing an emergent Leviathan to go unchained. If old limits were to be overstepped, new limits would have to be designed, new limits that might accomplish the reconciliation between the two conflicting social norms.

It is at this stage in our conjectural history that major mistakes seem to have been made, mistakes that apparently stemmed from a simple misunderstanding of economic principles. These mistakes, or apparent mistakes, have by this time become imbedded in our legal structure. Increasingly, legislatures and courts came to sanction collective or governmental interference with freedom of private contract, with the trading process, as such, while at the same time, they remained reluctant to sanction direct governmental transfers of endowments among persons. To economists, this result was, and is, essentially upside down. As noted earlier, intervention in the freedom of private persons to make contracts, to trade, must damage all parties. On the other hand and by contrast, a reassignment of endowments in premarket positions is, in the limit, a zero-sum transfer. At least one party gains what the other loses.

This is the origin of the continuing argument between economists and noneconomists over many particular proposals for governmental policy. Regardless of the distributive norms that they might hold, economists will tend to oppose overt interferences with voluntary contract. They will tend to oppose such measures as minimum wage legislation, price and wage controls, rent controls, gasoline rationing, marketing agreements, price supports, closed-shop restrictions, import and export quotas, direct bureaucratic allocations, and prohibitions. If they

share distributive norms with those who advance market intervention on such grounds, or if they accept the political necessity
of distributionally oriented policy, economists will tend to favor
direct transfers of income and wealth, welfare payments in cash
rather than in kind, positive and negative income taxation, and
wealth taxation. In taking such positions, the economists will,
quite correctly, be able to demonstrate that a larger pie, a larger
national dividend, will be produced by minimizing the interventions with market processes. Not only may any given set of
distributional norms be met more effectively; these norms may
even be exceeded if markets are allowed to function freely.

As I noted earlier, however, the economists have been too
ready to leave matters roughly at this point. They have been
unwilling to acknowledge that there may well be more in the
noneconomists' insistence on direct market intervention than
there appears to be in the economists' nonpolitical world. As
Knut Wicksell wisely pointed out nearly eighty years ago, most
economists talk as if they are advising a benevolent despot. But,
of course, such a despot is nonexistent. Governments embody
the choices and the actions of quite ordinary people, from
voters who exercise their ultimate political rights to franchise,
through legislative representatives who act for voters and for
themselves, to bureaucrats who actually carry out policy
decisions, including some of their own. The complex structure
that is government cannot readily be controlled at any level, and
any target is likely to be missed. Recognizing this, how is the
required reconciliation between political equality and private
property (individual freedom) to be secured? To go "whole hog"
with the economists on distributional policy, to open up
prospects for direct transfers of wealth among persons in
exchange for the enhanced efficiency promised by noninterven-
tion with market contract does not seem so attractive in this
setting. If government is to be used instrumentally to effect
direct transfers from "rich" to "poor," what is to prevent this
same instrumentality from being used by those in middle-income
and wealth coalitions from making direct transfers from others,
including the poor, to themselves? There is indeed evidence to
suggest that governmental distributional policy as it exists has
foundered on just such grounds (Stigler, 1970; Tullock, 1971).
If governmental transfer policy is acknowledged to be responsive

to the demands of citizens, who exercise their "public property rights" in the voting booth, there is nothing that will restrict this response to only those demands that are ethically motivated by some abstract norms. We cannot conceive of a constitutional rule or precept that would restrict the expression of individual and group interests to enforce consistency with "social values."

Perhaps working politicians, and judges, have shown some wisdom in their apparent reluctance to allow constitutional precepts to be adjusted in such a manner as to allow government to become a massive transfer process. These politicians may have realized that, in the net, the equivalent to transfers of wealth result from governmental activities. And they may also recognize that more direct transfers would increase overall economic efficiency. But here, as in other areas of human interaction, both hypocrisy and illusion may have virtues. By talking as if private property rights are enforceable by legal order while distributional objectives are being furthered by overt governmental interventions in market process, these politicians may have succeeded, up to a point, in distracting attention from the underlying contradiction that must be present. By making the market process the target for policy, they may have obscured the basic conflict that arises when premarket differences among persons in endowments, talents, and capacities to produce values coexist with political equality, defined in terms of voting franchise. By creating an illusion of action, political leaders may produce an acquiescence by potential voters in distributional differences that might otherwise not be tolerated. Hence, private property may be preserved, within limits, despite the potential power of political majorities.

Objection may be raised to my imputation of such sophistication to modern political leaders, but even if their motivations are wholly unconscious the model may retain behavioral content. If it does so, we may briefly look at some of its implications. We should predict that, despite the continuing plaints of the economists, specific and piecemeal intervention with voluntary contract would increase, with little or no desirable distributional consequences, despite the illusion of such results. We should predict continued journalistic and pseudo-philosophical attack on the market principle, as such, and on the institutional embodiments of this principle without the formulation of an effective organizational alternative. We should predict a rapidly expanding governmental sector, covering a widely varied set of activities and manned by an increasingly unwieldy and cumbersome bureaucratic apparatus.

THE WORLD WE LIVE IN

This description is, of course, one that fits the United States today. As an economist, I find this difficult to accept, even as the n-th best alternative. I am tempted to rally in support of my fellow professionals, those optimists who call for the enactment of universal negative income taxation in the hope that, once this legislation is on the books, we might be able to dismantle much of the grossly inefficient governmental structure that we currently observe. Only as a public-choice theorist, as an economist who has also done some thinking about how politics actually works, do I draw back here and realize that such is the stuff of utopian dreams. The introduction of the negative income tax would probably enhance rather than resolve the continuing contradiction.

If we lived in a world peopled by human beings who possessed roughly equal capacities to create values but who had been, by historical circumstances, forced into positions characterized by significant differences in nonhuman, physical property claims, reconciliation might be readily attainable. Conceptually, a once-and-for-all reassignment or redistribution of these nonhuman claims might be accomplished, after which the ideal setting for laissez-faire precepts would come into being. A regime of genuine classical liberalism might be within the realm of the imaginable. This is, of course, the world that was dreamed by the classical liberal philosophers, who did not acknowledge the existence of great capacity differences between themselves and the street porters. Unfortunately, history may suggest that Plato and not Adam Smith understood human differences. A major share of interpersonal endowment differentials may lie in the capacities to produce values, capacities that cannot be equalized by a reassignment of nonhuman assets or claims.

Where does this leave us? In a world where people are not, and cannot be, proximate "natural equals," how can the political equality that is both honored in precept and imbedded in institutional structure be reconciled with the differential rights of individuals to do things with things, the rights of private property? This is the question posed at the outset, and I have tried to explain some of the political behavior that we see in terms of responses to this question. The danger is, of course, that the continuation of current trends will reduce the attainment of both objectives. The attempted exercise of political equality may well produce an increase rather than a decrease in the inequalities among persons and families while, at the same time, reducing the freedom of individuals to dispose of their privately claimed rights. The differences in commands over final product values that we conceptually observe in the marketplace may seem intolerable in a society that gives more than lip service to political democracy. But it may be impossible to reduce these differences substantially without creating equally if not more intolerable differences in the power of individuals over each other. Even if she is motivated primarily by relative poverty, the call girl who sells services to one among many potential rich clients retains more freedom than the ordinary citizen who faces the monopoly bureaucrat. Interferences with markets, in the name of citizens, must be made by individuals who act on behalf of governments. The game is negative-sum over a wide range of weights assigned to individual freedom and to equality.

NOTES

1. Dissatisfaction with the distributive outcomes in a market economy has traditionally been central to the socialist critique of markets. For a sophisticated statement, see Dobb (1969, especially pp. 24–25). But the critique has by no means been limited to socialists. Many economists who support market organization acknowledge the validity of the socialist critique concerning distribution and implicitly suggest that the distributional outcomes observed are, in fact, attributable to the market process. James Meade is one of the few exceptions; he explicitly separates the distribution of ownership of property (the *premarket endowments distribution* in my terminology here) from the distribution of incomes that emerges from the market process, as such; see Meade (1965).

2. See my paper (Buchanan, 1971) for a discussion that introduces various models of equality among persons.

3. For a general discussion of how the several elements noted here may modify income distribution, see Friedman (1953).

4. The use of the Hobbesian model to analyze the potential emergence of a contract does not imply that, descriptively, the interaction among persons in anarchy need be close to that which Hobbes pictured. Behaviorally, persons might exhibit a wide range of traits. Nonetheless, as long as areas of conflict are present, there will be a basis for contractual agreement. There is no need at this level of discussion to specify just how much conflict Hobbesian anarchy would embody.

5. In this respect, much of modern economic theory is grossly misleading through its implication that trading outcomes are unique when there exist large numbers of both buyers and sellers. The uniqueness in the economists' models stems from the assumptions made about potential recontracting in a timeless process that converges to equilibrium, assumptions that are not remotely descriptive of any trading process as observed.

6. This term was introduced by Winston Bush; see Bush (1972).

7. As Gordon Tullock's appropriately titled essay "The Edge of the Jungle" suggests, civil order always exists alongside potential Hobbesian conflict; see Tullock (1972).

8. This name is helpful in distinguishing the *Enforcer State* from its complement, that State which provides goods and services publicly, which may be called the *Productive State*.

9. Even in this restrictive context, political action can insure some net redistribution, provided that the public sector is sufficiently large relative to the private sector. Where collective or public goods and services are equally available to all consumers, the efficient structure of prices may well involve income wealth-related differentials. If, however, an attempt is made to move beyond these efficiency limits in public goods pricing (that is, if redistributive norms are introduced directly into the fiscal process), the due process clause would be violated on a strict interpretation.

REFERENCES

Buchanan, J. M. (1971) "Equality as Fact and Norm," *Ethics*, 81 (April), 228–240.

Buchanan, J. M. (1975) *The Limits of Liberty: Between Anarchy and Leviathan*. Chicago: The University of Chicago Press.

Bush, W. C. (1972) "Individual Welfare in Anarchy," in G. Tullock, ed., *Explorations in the Theory of Anarchy*. Blacksburg, Va.: Center for Study of Public Choice.

Dobb, M. (1969) *Welfare Economics and the Economics of Socialism*. Cambridge: Cambridge University Press.

Friedman, M. (1953) "Choice, Chance, and the Personal Distribution of Income," *Journal of Political Economy*, 61 (August), 277–290.

Meade, J. E. (1965) *Efficiency, Equity, and the Ownership of Property.* Cambridge, Mass.: Harvard University Press.

Stigler, G. (1970) "Director's Law of Public Income Redistribution," *Journal of Law and Economics*, 13 (April), 1-10.

Tullock, G. (1971) "The Charity of the Uncharitable," *Western Economic Journal*, 9 (December), 379-392.

Tullock, G. (1972) "The Edge of the Jungle," in G. Tullock, ed., *Explorations in the Theory of Anarchy.* Blacksburg, Va.: Center for Study of Public Choice.

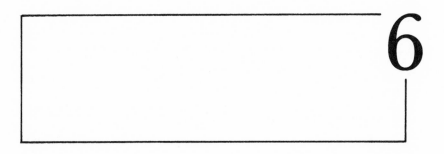

GOVERNMENT EXPENDITURES: CASH OR IN-KIND AID?

LESTER C. THUROW

Massachusetts Institute of Technology

In neoclassical economic theory, government expenditures serve two functions. First, they provide certain types of collective goods, called pure public goods, that cannot be provided in private markets. Second, they alter the distribution of income. In this second role, neoclassical economic theory concludes that cash dominates in-kind aid. Once an optimum distribution of income has been established, governments are to stand aside and allow consumer sovereignty plus competitive markets to work. In a federal system, the ideal system of cash transfers would consist of three parts: from the federal government to state and local governments, from the federal government to individuals, and from the state and local governments to individuals. The result would be an optimum distribution of income within each area, with individuals free to make their own expenditure decisions. Any further intervention can be "shown" to lower consumer utility below what it otherwise could be. If the individual is forced to buy or is given goods, less utility is the result. Hence, cash is more efficient than in-kind aid.

While there is an admitted case for in-kind government expenditures when the goods in question are "pure public" goods, most domestic expenditures do not meet the necessary qualifications. Pure public goods have three characteristics that prevent them from being sold in private markets. Each of these characteristics is easiest to see in the area of national defense—the paradigm case of a pure public good. First, exclusion is impossible. If I have national defense protection, my neighbor has national defense protection. Second, consumption is nonrival. My neighbor's enjoyment of national defense does not subtract from my enjoyment. Third, identical amounts must be consumed. My neighbor and I must agree on a common defense expenditure.

All three of these characteristics lead to the problem of revealed preferences. We will not reveal our preferences and agree to pay for defense voluntarily in the same manner that we pay for television sets. Each of us has an incentive to hide our desires for national defense. We will get approximately the same amount of defense, but pay less. The result, then, is too little expenditure on defense, in relation to our own preferences. As a result, national defense cannot be sold as if it were television sets, and governments must be involved in its purchase. Most domestic government expenditures, however, go for goods that can be, and are, sold privately (education, health care, housing, recreation, transportation, for example).

Since domestic expenditures are not pure public goods, this brings us back to the perception that cash dominates restricted grants in domestic affairs. But how valid is this conclusion and the assumptions upon which it is based? If the perception is not correct, where should the line be drawn between the use of cash and restricted transfers? These are the questions that this chapter seeks to investigate.

PARETO OPTIMALITY

Most of the existing economic literature analyzes the problem of government expenditures from the point of view of "Pareto optimality."[1] (Pareto optimality exists when no one in the society can be made better off without someone else being made worse off.) The potential donor (also called in this chapter the taxpayer and individual 1) and the potential donee (also the expenditure recipient and individual 2) both have utility functions that they wish to maximize, subject to an initial exogenous budget constraint. To justify transfers, the donee's utility or consumption of some particular good appears in the utility function of the donor (see Eqs. 1 and 2). To generate interdependent utility functions, some external benefit is hypothesized to flow from the donee's utility or consumption to the donor.

$$U^1 = f_1(Y^1, X_2^1, \ldots, X_n^1, U^2) \tag{1}$$

$$U^1 = f_2(Y^1, X_2^1, \ldots, X_n^1, C_1^2) \tag{2}$$

where

U^1 = utility of individual 1

Y^1 = income of individual 1

$X_2^1, \ldots, X_n^1$ = nonmarket goods of individual 1

U^2 = utility of individual 2

C_1^2 = consumption of good 1 by individual 2

The existence of an external benefit can lead to either an explanation of private charity or an argument for governmental intervention. If individual 1 is the only person to receive more utility when the utility or consumption of individual 2 rises, then individual 1 must decide whether it is worthwhile to make a charitable contribution to individual 2. If the interrelationships of utility functions are such that many individuals, not just individual 1, gain utility when the utility or consumption of individual 2 rises, then the external benefit, but not the expenditure itself, has the characteristics of a pure public good. Many people benefit from the same expenditure, which leads to a problem of who should pay for it. The government must become involved because private charity will not lead to enough transfers relative to the preferences of the potential givers. Too few resources will be transferred since each individual expects to gain the benefits of the transfers without having to pay for them.[2]

Viewed from the donee's perspective, unrestricted cash transfers maximize utility (see Eq. 3).

$$U^2 = (Y^2, X_2^2, \ldots, X_n^2) \tag{3}$$

where Y^2 = cash income of individual 2

$X_2^2, \ldots, X_n^2$ = nonmarket goods of individual 2

From the point of view of Pareto optimality, however, the preferences of individual 2—the donee—do not count in establishing any system of voluntary transfers. Only the preferences of the donor count. Maximizing the donor's utility depends upon the exact interdependence of the utility functions.

If the donee's utility appears in the donor's utility functions, then cash transfers also maximize the donor's utility. The donee is best able to determine what maximizes his own utility. If the externality flows from some particular good, then the donor has two options in maximizing his utility per dollar of transfer. He can give cash transfers and take advantage of the donee's *income elasticity of demand* for the targeted good or he can give a restricted grant (in the form of either vouchers or subsidized in-kind provision) that takes advantage of his *price elasticity of demand* for the targeted good.[3] In the first case, the donor relies on the fact that the donee will voluntarily purchase more of the desired good with an increased income, and inclination measured by the income elasticity of demand. In the second case, the donor relies on the fact that the donee will voluntarily purchase more of the desired good as the price of the good falls, a propensity measured by the price elasticity of demand. Since operating via the price elasticity of demand is always cheaper than operating via the income elasticity of demand, *restricted transfers always dominate unrestricted transfers when the interdependence flows from the consumption of a particular good.*

As a result, it is not true that cash grants always dominate restricted grants in neoclassical economics. In the case of interdependence flowing from specific goods and services, restricted grants dominate cash grants. This conclusion then raises the empirical question of whether individuals receive utility (happiness?) when a neighbor's utility rises or when the neighbor's consumption of some particular good and service increases. If a taxpayer receives utility from the consumption of a neighbor's housing, medical care, or education, and not from that neighbor's utility, then these services should be provided directly to the taxpayer.

It is interesting, however, that the economics literature that reached these results is unwilling to draw the conclusion that follows from its own analysis. Sometimes explicitly, and even more often implicitly, the Pareto optimality literature makes the judgment that a "rational" donor should be interested only in the donee's utility.[4] To want to specify the consumption of some particular good or service is to be "irrational" and in the world of the "second best." In reaching this conclusion, it is the economist who is being irrational while imposing personal value judgments. From the point of view of Pareto optimality, there is no such thing as an irrational preference. If some expenditure yields utility, it yields utility, and the individual who spends money for that purpose is rational.

While from the point of view of Pareto optimality there are no irrational preferences, the explicit or implicit judgment of irrationality is understandable, since the term *externality* has been expanded so that it has become a tautological explanation for everything and anything that is done. Consequently, it has lost its meaning and become a satisfactory explanation for nothing. To be a useful explanation of why utility functions are interdependent, the term *externality* must be limited to real, measurable phenomena, such as sociological (e.g., less crime), political (e.g., better voters), or economic (e.g., lower food prices). When *externality* is used as a vague label for some unspecified psychic income received by the donor, it ceases to have any explanatory power. We know only that psychic income externalities exist when government transfers or expenditures exist. Used in this way, psychic income is not an explanation of why individuals are interested in the education, housing, and medical care of other citizens, but is merely another way of describing an apparent interest.

The concept of external benefits just is not a convincing explanation of most domestic public expenditures. Consider a few examples of some of the most important public expenditures. Medical care does not generate externalities once a society gets beyond basic public health measures and communicable diseases. Death is the most private of all activities. There are no nonmarket economic effects on the general population; it is inevitable in any case. Similarly, arguments that education generates externalities are unconvincing once one gets beyond elementary education (literacy, etc.).[5] Basic research may generate externalities, but the effects of research can be separated from those of education, even if they often occur in the same institutions. Neighborhood externalities certainly exist in housing (the price of any house in a neighborhood depends to a great extent on the quality of the other houses in the neighborhood), but the neighborhood externalities do not lead to the types of programs that have been legislated. Government programs have focused on national minimum housing standards for each family and not on common levels of maintenance, or lack of it, where each neighborhood decides on its own level of maintenance. Fire protection is like medical care in that some limited amount of fire protection and code enforcement is necessary to prevent conflagrations, but beyond this, a donor has no more interest in the fire protection of neighbors than in their fire insurance.[6] Police protection can be described as preventing externalities, but it may more sensibly be thought of as enforcing the rules of the economic game (a subject to which we shall return).

By attempting to escape into the concept of externalities, economists have avoided facing the fact that individuals do seem to have preferences about their neighbors' consumption of particular goods and services. Many reasons could be advanced as to why and how such preferences came about (I may be for equal health care since such a policy insures that I will get equal health care if I need it), but the reasons for the preferences are basically irrelevant. The only relevant fact is whether such preferences do or do not exist. If they do exist, there is a Pareto optimality argument for restricted transfers targeted at particular goods.

SOCIAL WELFARE FUNCTIONS

While its development is less recent, the major technique for analyzing economic welfare is not Pareto optimality, but social welfare functions. Social welfare functions are mathematical expressions showing the relationships between social welfare and the different factors that create social welfare. They stand in the same relationship to a society as utility functions do to an individual.

The most commonly used social welfare function is the individualistic social welfare function. In it, social welfare is some weighted average of individual utilities (see Eq. 4).

$$SW = f(U^1, U^2, \ldots, U^m) \qquad (4)$$

where SW = social welfare

$U^1, U^2, \ldots, U^m$ = utility of society's members

The individualistic social welfare function always leads to cash transfers rather than to in-kind aid. Interpersonal comparisons that raise or lower individual budget constraints may be made, but as long as utility appears as the sole argument in the social welfare function, cash transfers dominate restricted transfers. Individuals may determine their own utility, and cash always produces at least as much utility for donees as do restricted transfers. Other people may have a role in determining the weight (form of the function) attached to each individual utility, but they have no role in determining the utility itself.

While the individualistic social welfare function unambiguously leads to cash grants, there is an open question as to whether the individualistic social welfare function is an adequate representation of social welfare judgments. Its inadequacies can be seen in the problem of determining the proper weights or functional form. How are these weights to be determined? There is no answer. Yet, the weights and functional forms are necessary for making social welfare judgments. In keeping with the spirit of the individualistic social welfare function, individual preferences should play a role in determining the weights or functional form of the social welfare function. This, however, leads to individuals who have two different levels of preferences—about what yields them utility and about the appropriate weights to assign to different utilities in the social welfare function.

This distinction leads to possible modifications in the individualistic social welfare function. Individual preferences can be separated into those that concern the ideal rules of the economic game (such as communism and capitalism) and the optimum distribution of economic prizes (such as social welfare function weights) and those that concern the maximization of personal utility within any given economic game or distribution of prizes. Occurring at different levels, these preferences can differ from each other without being logically self-contradictory. For example, there is nothing self-contradictory in seeking to become extremely wealthy and powerful in our current economic game, yet believing that a better one would award no "extremely wealthy" prizes. The two preferences simply do not exist in the same domain.

To distinguish these two levels of preferences, I call the one *individual-societal preferences* and the other *private-personal preferences.*[7] This distinction makes it possible to avoid some of the problems inherent in individualistic social welfare functions. Societies can, if they wish, discuss what constitutes economic equity without worrying about differences in the efficiency with which people process economic goods (the miser does not need to be given transfers only on the basis of being a miser and, hence, receiving more utility per dollar). A preference such as envy is ruled out, not because it does not exist and not because it does not affect private-personal utility (it does), but because society chooses not to take envy into account in its social rules, even though each one of its members may be envious. In their individual-societal preferences, individuals decide to rule out the private-personal preferences of envy since, collectively, it can lead to absurd results (zero incomes for everyone, for example).

One of the implications of individual-societal preferences is that our social welfare function may include arguments other than individual utilities. It might, for example, directly include the distribution of medical care, housing, or education (see Eq. 5).

$$SW = f(U^1, \ldots, U^m, dM, dH, dE) \qquad (5)$$

where dM = distribution of medical care
  dH = distribution of housing
  dE = distribution of education

These arguments are there not because they maximize private-personal utility, but because they reflect individual-societal preferences.

But what are our individual-societal preferences about the structure of the economic game and the distribution of economic prizes? Obviously, I do not have the definitive empirical answer to this question. I would argue, however, that the optimum rules of the economic game are to be found, not in the factors that generate private-personal utility, but in the factors that generate individual-societal social welfare. Individual-societal preferences are those preferences that individuals are willing to elevate into general rules of the economic game. Basically, this means the analysis of those abstract phrases that most of us agree should specifically determine these rules (for example, the good society, human rights, equal opportunity). While there may be disagreements on what these phrases imply about the rules, such as whether they include an equal right to health care, most of us probably agree that an equal distribution of voting rights (access to public expenditures and taxes) is implied, while we also probably agree that an equal distribution of fountain pens is not implied.

Concerns about fountain pens are ruled out, not only because no one happens to have individual–societal preferences vis-à-vis fountain pens, but because no one can show a route of linkage between fountain pens and social goals (such as equal opportunity). The real problem is not in dealing with such *reducto ad absurdum* logical possibilities, but in analysis of the gray areas of disagreement.

Health care is a good example of the different types of analysis that would spring from private-personal preferences and individual–societal preferences. I would argue, for example, that society's interest in the distribution of medical care springs, not from unspecified externalities that affect private-personal utility, but from our individual–societal preferences that "human rights" include an *equal* "right" to health care. If you like, we may want to live in a society that is communistic with respect to health care rights. Because of private-personal utility blinders, economists act as if it is irrational for a society to desire an equal distribution of medical care, yet perfectly rational for society to be communistic with respect to political voting power (one person, one vote) or all economic goods and services. The same reasoning that leads us to equality in voting rights might lead us to equality in medical care rights. Because of this desire, a society may wish not only to establish some minimum standard of medical care but also to equalize medical care—just as there are desires to equalize voting power and not to ensure that everyone has some minimum quantity of voting power. To be for equalized distribution of health care and for some degree of unequalized distribution of other economic goods and services is not to be internally inconsistent. An equal distribution of general purchasing power may not be part of your conception of human rights. *To have equality in the distribution of medical care and still permit inequality in the distribution of general goods and services, it is necessary to provide a voucher or in-kind distribution of medical services.*

Similar arguments could be made for education and housing. Restricted transfer of these commodities springs not from externalities but from our individual-societal preferences as to what constitutes a good society. Compulsory education says that human rights include the right and *the duty* to acquire some minimum level of education, not because it maximizes the recipient's private-personal utility, but because it maximizes the individual-societal welfare of both the donor and the donee. As a result, restricted transfers flow, not from interdependent private-personal utility functions, but from our individual-societal preferences and the resulting social welfare function. In this social welfare function, the equal distribution of the right to medical care and the consequent distribution of such care may be a direct argument.

Musgrave (1959, p. 13) has labeled such goods *merit wants*, but the term is slightly misleading. The key factor is not that individuals merit some quantity of these goods (they also merit some quantity of goods and services in general if no one is allocated a zero income in the distribution of income), but that these goods appear as direct arguments in society's social welfare function and are to be distributed in a manner different from that of goods and services in general.

Given different optimum distributions for different goods, governments are faced with a problem. One distribution of money income is not capable of producing two different distributions of goods and services. If, on the one hand, the general income distribution is used to meet a social goal of equal medical care, then incomes must be equally distributed. This leaves general goods and services "too equally" distributed. If, on the other hand, the general income distributed is used to generate the desired distribution of general goods and services, medical care will be "too unequally" distributed. The problem is the classic one of too many goals and not enough policy instruments.

Practically speaking, governments must provide for the general distribution of goods and services through the distribution of income, and provide for the distribution of merit wants in other ways, usually meaning governments' public provision in-kind. There is an intermediate option of creating a second type of money (red money, chits, vouchers, whatever) that can be used only to purchase particular goods and services. This second type of money can then be distributed to generate the desired distribution for the particular goods or services in question. Market suppliers ultimately trade their red money or vouchers for normal green money.

Education voucher plans fall into this category. Governments pay for some minimum quantity of a child's education by issuing each child a voucher worth some amount, but these vouchers can (and must) be used to purchase education at whatever school the student and the parents think most appropriate. The public pays, but it does not provide.

If the good or service in question is one that society is not particularly interested in completely equalizing, governments can allow its purchase with both red money and green money. The equal distribution of red money guarantees that each person receives a minimum quantity of goods and services. The distribution of green money allows the purchase of more than this minimum, if desired. If the good or service is one that society wants equalized, then governments must prevent the purchase of such goods and services with green money. Only the distribution of red money is allowed to determine the ultimate distribution of the good in question.[8]

What factors determine whether merit wants should be provided directly by the government or indirectly by the issue of special money? The answer lies in the level of detail of individual–societal preferences. Since it seems doubtful that individual–societal preferences generally extend down to the detailed characteristics of the goods or services in question, voucher systems would seem to dominate in-kind provision in most cases. A society may, for example, have social norms concerning minimum housing standards without having preferences about the detailed characteristics of the housing. The lack of such preferences argues for vouchers to allow each person to decide detailed housing characteristics for himself or herself.

In any event, if a more general approach is taken to social welfare functions, restricted transfers cannot be categorically ruled out as they are in the individualistic social welfare function. Restricted transfers may be necessary to maximize social welfare if particular goods appear as direct arguments in the social welfare function.

LIMITED CONSUMER SOVEREIGNTY

At the heart of the economist's love affair with cash transfers is the doctrine of absolute consumer sovereignty. Individuals are the most qualified judges of how to best maximize their own utility. Real public policies must face up to a modification of this simplistic view—there are individuals who are incompetent to make their own decisions. Historically and legally we have tried to deal with the problem of incompetence by dichotomizing the population into those who are legally incompetent to make any and all decisions (minors and institutionalized persons) and the remaining population, who are presumed competent to make any and all decisions.

Increasingly, we are coming to recognize that these divisions cannot be made so distinct. There is a continuum of individuals ranging from those who are entirely competent to those who are entirely incompetent. Halfway houses, drug rehabilitation centers, and their equivalent are being established for criminals, mental patients, the mentally retarded, drug addicts, etc. Obviously it is a difficult problem to establish any individual's degree of incompetence, but the existence of incompetence is a problem that neither governments nor economists can ignore.[9]

Governments have a whole range of public policies that can be used to supplement or supplant consumer sovereignty, but one of the mildest and least coercive of these is the public provision of goods and services in-kind. Such in-kind aid can be used to influence individuals to make those decisions that society thinks they would be making if they fell into those classes with absolute consumer sovereignty.

The extent of the problems created by limited consumer sovereignty are expanded by differences in personal management efficiency. How good is the family in managing and providing the normal housekeeping functions that each family provides in-kind to itself? Economists act as though every family's efficiency were equally superb. Realistically, there is a continuum of family management ability. As a result the same cash income will provide different "real" standards of living for different families.

Suppose that society has a general income distribution objective that calls for some minimum real standard of living. Does it set its cash transfers at a level where the best family manager, the average family manager, or the worst family manager can reach the desired minimum?[10] Given the probable range in management inefficiencies, the cash transfers that would be necessary to hold every family at some minimum real standard of living (in spite of its own inefficiencies) would be impossibly large. Practically speaking, there is no way to adjust income transfer payments to the level of each family's management efficiency. As a result, simple efficiency calls for constraining family management inefficiencies with in-kind aid. Economists deal with efficiency differences between firms by relying on the sacred right of the inefficient to fail, but this is clearly an inadequate response to inefficient families. One of the key reasons for our general interest in minimum standards of living and cash transfers is our desire to prevent "failing" families.

The real-world continuum between those with no consumer sovereignty and those with absolute consumer sovereignty and the real-world interest in preventing family failures both lead to a public interest in the question of where individuals fall on the continuum between those with no decision-making competence and those with absolute decision-making competence. Given this determination, it then becomes possible to ask how income transfer payments or the public in-kind provision can rectify limited consumer sovereignty and prevent family management failures.

Generally, the individual or the family needs decision-making aid and not some particular consumption good or service. The latter can be purchased. The purchase of "decision aiders," however, does not seem to be a possibility. Decision aiders are available in the private market (investment consultants are the best example), but decision-making competence is necessary to purchase a good decision aider and this is exactly the quality that has been called into question. Limited consumer sovereignty, and the limited "right to fail," would call for the public in-kind provision of decision-aiding or decision-making services.

Governments need not provide drug treatment centers, but they must provide the services of someone advising or, if necessary, requiring such treatment. Correspondingly, governments do not need to provide groceries, but they may need to provide an advisor for families who want to achieve some minimum of family management efficiency or, if necessary, to require some minimum of family efficiency. Given the desire to respect consumer sovereignty as much as possible, the primary focus would be on decision-aiding services to be supplemented by decision-making services when the former have clearly failed.

The only exceptions spring from limitations on the right of an individual or a family to fail. If some abnormally expensive item is necessary to stop an individual from failing (drug rehabilitation, for example), the necessary service may need to be provided in-kind and cannot be paid for from general income-transfer payments (they won't be large enough). If the necessary purchase is involuntary and will be made only under compulsion, in-kind public provision is probably the only feasible solution. Private markets are just not set up to handle involuntary purchases.

Given a continuum of individuals with varying degrees of competence, transfer systems need a corresponding continuum of transfers ranging from cash, cash with advice, vouchers, in-kind provision, and, finally, compulsion. Efficiency may also call for in-kind provision in cases where cash would work, but only with large expenditures relative to in-kind aid.

THE CREATION OF INDIVIDUAL VALUES

Part of the mythology of economics is the proposition that innate consumer preferences exist fully grown in each individual and that values flow from the individual to society, not in the reverse direction. Basically, from the economics point of view, people are machines with innate desires, who derive satisfaction from processing sets of inputs (consumption goods). Individuals are best able to judge their own welfare. They usually want to be better off than they are. When all people are prosperous, then society also gains.

What the simple model of "homo economicus" fails to confront is the process whereby individual wants, preferences, or values are created. Given modern sociology and psychology, the postulate of static, innate wants is simply untenable. Every society has always implicitly affected the wants of its population. As biological needs receded, sociological needs increased. As a result, it is no longer possible to maintain the fiction that the American society responds to individual desires but does not create them. We must now explicitly recognize what we have always done implicitly.

John K. Galbraith (1969, p. 131) has repeatedly skirted this problem by noting that there may be a bias against public goods because they are not advertised as extensively as private goods. He makes two mistakes. First, advertising is only one of several important methods for creating wants. Second, he implies that such advertising distorts individual preferences. The real problem is not the distortion of innate wants, but the fact that wants are generated by social pressures. There are no innate wants (other than the biological ones) to which we can appeal or to which we can return.

Directly and indirectly, American society generates the wants of American individuals. With overt persuasion, purchases will differ from what they would have been, but they will be in accordance with current preferences. What is more, the new desires have the same validity as the old ones—both were socially determined. The only difference is that some desires may be more consciously created than others.

Although Americans have always used private and governmental persuasion to create the desired wants (such as belief in democracy), overt persuasion has always been associated with totalitarian dictatorships. This polarized association is unfortunate since it obscures the real problem—not whether wants are going to be socially generated (they are), but what techniques of overt and covert persuasion are to be allowed. To what extent should the education system be used to inculcate values? Is subliminal advertising permissible? How much peer group pressure is allowable? These are the real questions that must be answered. To be against dictatorship does not solve the problem.

While we often imagine the polar totalitarian extreme, the problem can be put in perspective by imagining the opposite extreme. What would society look like if there were no social persuasion? With no commonly shared beliefs and wants, anarchy would result. Any society would be impossible.

The relevant question is what degree of governmental persuasion should be used in inculcating values? If societies did not believe in creating and enforcing values, laws and police departments would be unnecessary. People would operate on their own values. Enforcing the rules of the game is not simply a matter of force, however. It is also a matter of establishing the belief that these rules are correct.

What role should the public provision of goods and services play in the creation of individual values? Viewed as a problem in literacy, educational vouchers may dominate public schools, but viewed as value creation, public schools may well dominate educational vouchers. Public schools allow society to ensure that each individual will be inculcated with, or at least exposed to, the basic values of society. Whether this is necessary or unnecessary obviously depends on expectations as to what values would be established in private schools. No democracy, for example, could survive a fascist school system.

Another example exists in the area of drug rehabilitation. A simple application of neoclassical economic principles would allow a free market in hard drugs, give each person the right to become a drug addict, permit individuals who wish it to commit suicide, and interfere only to prevent drug addicts from intruding on the activities of the rest of the population. Yet society seeks to alter the actions of the actual or potential drug addict, not because these are antisocial actions that harm others, but because any society requires positive commitments to its values as well as the absence of negative externalities.

As a result, it is necessary to ask what values American society holds so deeply, and which of them are so fundamental to it, that it wants government programs to inculcate these values in each of its citizens. What beliefs are so basic that society does not want to leave it to the accidental forces of the marketplace to determine whether individuals are or are not exposed to them?

If there are any such beliefs, and I suspect that there are, then it is necessary to ask how the in-kind provision of services can contribute to propagating the desired values. The current disputes over child care are a good illustration of the problem. For example, if public child care is designed to allow each mother an equal opportunity to go to work (regardless of her husband's income), then vouchered, private child-care centers may be the appropriate answer. If child-care centers are also desired as a method of altering values and characteristics ("enrichment" is our current euphemism), then public in-kind provision of child care is appropriate. If society wants to change the values that the mothers would inculcate if they were at home, it obviously cannot allow the mothers to pick the private child-care centers that the public funds are to support. (In either case, however, restricted transfers dominate cash.)

No amount of cash income redistribution can solve the value creation problem. When a society thinks that some value is so important that everyone should have it, in-kind provision of some good or service is apt to occur as part of the system of transmitting the desired value.

DIVERGENT PERSPECTIVES

Often societies and individuals will differ as to the cost-benefit calculus for human investment projects. This comes about, not because they are working with a different set of objective facts, but because of divergent perspectives. The differences are apt to occur principally in the areas of risk preferences and time discounting.

A low-income individual who is subject to severe budget constraints must have a high rate of time preference in order to allocate limited funds in accordance with economic rationality. To give up today's use of economic resources, the person must receive a high rate of return. In other words, no amount of interest will persuade a person who is starving to death today to eat some food now and some tomorrow, for death could be the result. A rational starving person has an infinite rate of time preference. Society, however, with its higher per capita income may have a very different rate of time preference. It may come to the conclusion that a particular training program is a good investment, while at the same time the individual decides that it is personally not a good investment.

Similarly, risk preferences may differ substantially. Since society has the benefit of large numbers and a large budget constraint, it can be expected to operate on an expected-value basis when making investment decisions. Individuals, however, are much more apt to be averse to risk. They do not have the benefit of large numbers, and their investment expenditures are apt to be large in relation to their own resources. Consider the common conclusion that a college education generates a 10 percent rate of return for white males. This calculation may be entirely correct, but it ignores the variance in earnings among both college and high school males. Approximately 28 percent of all college-educated white males end up earning less than the average high school–educated white male. Conversely, 21 percent of all high school–educated white males end up earning more than the average college-educated white male (Bureau of the Census, 1972). When the foregone earnings and costs of acquiring a college education are considered, one should keep in mind that there is an associated failure risk of over 60 percent (where white males are concerned). It might be perfectly rational for these individuals to avoid investing in a college education because of the high degree of risk, yet, on the average, there is a 10 percent rate of return.

The only solution is to bring individual cost–benefit calculations into line with social cost–benefit calculations. Technically, this would lead to a set of subsidizers (vouchers or in-kind aid) that would bring the average individual cost–benefit calculation into line with the social cost–benefit calculations. Once again, however, there is a case to be made for restricted aid.

DISTRIBUTION AND MARKETING COSTS

While exclusion is technically possible with most domestic government expenditures, the argument is often made that the costs of exclusion are so high that the good should not be provided in private markets. Distribution and marketing costs are so high relative to production costs that the goods should be given away at the public's expense. Roads are the common example. Tolls are collected on many roads and bridges and could, in principle, be collected on all roads. It is much more efficient (less costly), however, to collect road tolls at the gasoline pump in the form of an excise tax. The goods seem to be provided free to the users, but they actually pay for them with a benefit tax.

Old age and medical insurance are sometimes advanced as examples of the same phenomenon. The costs of selling private insurance are typically very high relative to the benefits paid (the production costs). As a result, it is cheaper to sell old age and medical insurance in the form of a benefit tax and to provide the goods through the public sector.

The only problem with this principle is that there are clearly many goods whose selling costs are high relative to their production costs. Yet, most of us would not want to make every good with high selling costs into a public good. Thus, there must be some principle other than high distribution costs that makes some goods private and others public. Therefore, I would argue that high exclusion and marketing costs are not a basic argument for public provision.

SECOND-BEST ARGUMENTS

Recently, my colleague Martin Weitzman (1974) developed an argument for the public provision of goods and services in the second-best world of nonoptimal income distributions. He is able to show that under certain circumstances, rationing dominates the price system as a mechanism for maximizing utility. The model is the standard one—each individual has a *utility function* and social welfare is the simple summation of individual utilities. The optimal distribution of income is the one that maximizes utility. An egalitarian distribution of income is assumed to be optimal.

Given a distribution of tastes (strength of preferences for particular goods and services) and incomes, it is possible to work out the price system distribution of goods and services and compare it with the results of an egalitarian rationing system.

When tastes are widely dispersed and incomes are distributed relatively equally (close to the optimum), the price system dominates the rationing system in generating utility. When tastes are relatively equally distributed and incomes are unequally distributed, the rationing system dominates the price system in generating utility.

While the particular definition of an optimum distribution of income used in this chapter increases the probability that rationing will dominate the price mechanism, it does not produce the result. Basically, the same result holds whenever the actual distribution of income is farther away from the optimal distribution of income than is the rationing distribution of income.

While the best public policy (creating the optimum distribution of income) dominates the second-best policy, there is an argument for the public provision of general goods and services in a second-best world.

CONCLUSION

Where does this leave us with respect to drawing the line between cash and restricted transfers? As this chapter has shown, it is not axiomatically true that cash transfers dominate restricted transfers. Even within the framework of neoclassical economics, the results depend upon the precise nature of the individual utility function and the social welfare function. Outside the framework of neoclassical economics, limitations on consumer sovereignty, interest in preventing family failures, and the problem of creating values can all lead to restricted transfers. Second-best arguments can be advanced.

At the same time, the basic case for not intervening in other people's spending decisions is strong enough that the burden of proof should always lie on those advocating restricted grants. It is their duty to show that the aid flows from specific good interdependencies, that it is an argument in our social welfare function, that it is directed at groups with limited consumer sovereignty, that it will promote essential values, or that it is a legitimate second-best policy.

Given this burden of proof, I suspect that we will find many goods that are now given in-kind that should not be and some goods that are not given in-kind that should be. I, for one, find the specific case for in-kind housing assistance unconvincing, but the arguments for an equal distribution of medical services overwhelming.

There is also the problem of whether the restricted transfers should be given in the form of in-kind public goods and services or in the form of vouchers and alternative distributions of purchasing power. Here again, the burden of proof should rest with those advocating public in-kind aid rather than vouchers. The least possible interference with individual preferences is good principle, even if it is not always an overriding one.

NOTES

1. For two of many examples see Pauly (1970) and Hockman and Rodgers (1969).

2. Total demand curves would be determined by the horizontal addition of direct demand curves and by the vertical addition of indirect (externalities) demand curves.

3. For an optimum system of subsidies, using both price and income elasticities, see Thurow (1966).

4. For an explicit example see Tullock and Olsen (1971).

5. For an attempt to specify the externalities that flow from education see Weisbrod (1964).

6. Economy of scale arguments do not make fire protection into a public good any more than they make electricity generation and distribution into a public good.

7. For a longer discussion of the two types of preferences see Thurow (1973).

8. The need to prevent resale for green money is one of the arguments that can be made for in-kind provision as opposed to voucher provision.

9. Governments must be involved since no individual can have the right to declare some other individual incompetent.

10. This is not an argument that the poor are on the average worse managers than the rich but simply an argument that there is a range of management abilities in all income classes. Mismanagement is simply more significant if you are poor.

REFERENCES

Bureau of the Census (1972). *Current Population Reports: Consumer Income, 1971. Washington, D.C.: Government Printing Office (No. 124).*

Galbraith, J. K. (1969). *The Affluent Society.* Boston: Houghton Mifflin.

Hockman, H., and Rodgers, J. (1969). "Pareto Optimal Redistributions," *American Economic Review*, 59(4), pt. 1, 542-557.

Musgrave, R. A. (1959). *The Theory of Public Finance.* New York: McGraw-Hill.

Pauly, M. (1970). "Efficiency in the Provision of Consumption Subsidies," *Kyklos*, 23, 33-57.

Thurow, L. C., (1966). "The Theory of Grants-In-Aid," *National Tax Journal*, 19(4), 373-377.

Thurow, L. C. (1973). "Toward a Definition of Economic Justice," *The Public Interest*, 31, 56-80.

Tullock, G., and Olsen, E. O. (1971). "Subsidized Housing in a Competitive Market," *American Economic Review*, 61(1), 218-224.

Weisbrod, B. (1964). *External Benefits of Public Education.* Princeton: Princeton University Press.

Weitzman, M. (1974). *Is the Price System or Rationing More Effective in Getting a Commodity to Those Who Need It?* MIT Working Paper, Cambridge, Mass: Massachusetts Institute of Technology. (January, 1974).

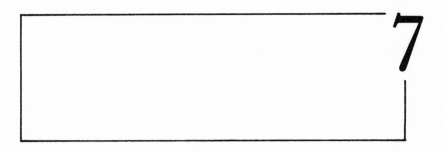

LABOR, LEISURE, AND A DISTINCTIVE CONTRADICTION OF ADVANCED CAPITALISM

GERALD A. COHEN
London University

In this chapter, I draw attention to the classical and Marxian distinction between use-value and exchange-value, and I show how the relation between them under capitalism generates a peculiar contradiction when capitalism is advanced.

A contradiction obtains when a society's economic organization frustrates the optimal use and development of its accumulated productive power, when possibilities opened by its productive forces are closed by its production relations. I take the term *contradiction* from Marx's Preface to his *Critique of Political Economy* (Marx and Engels, 1958), and I intend no connection between my use of it and the meaning it has in logic:

> At a certain stage of their development, the material productive forces of society come into contradiction with the existing relations of production. . . . From forms of development of the productive forces these relations turn into their fetters. (p. 363)[1]

The concept of advanced capitalism will be clarified by the exposition of its contradiction, on page 116. It will prove plausible to assert that at least American capitalism is advanced in the appropriate sense. This chapter offers an indictment of that society based on considerations wholly independent of its severe domestic inequality and imperialist world posture.[2] These factors would condemn it even if the United States were a society of substantial equality, isolated from the rest of the world.

The capitalist essence is at issue here, not the accidents of geography and history. Advanced capitalism as I discuss it relates to contemporary American capitalism, as the capitalism of *Capital* does to Victorian British capitalism. In each case the consequences of principles animating the society are explored *in abstracto*; but the results bear on reality, since the animating principles are really there (cf. Marx, 1962, p. 141).

The initial sections of this chapter define five concepts that figure in the portrayal of capitalism: *use-value, commodity, exchange-value, money,* and *capital.* The definitions purport to codify Marx's usual conceptual practice, but they do not accommodate his every employment of the terms. Marx used concepts clearly, yet not so carefully as to determine unique definitions of them. It is my aim to be simple and precise and generally faithful to his ideas. As much as possible, I ignore complications; but some further discussion of the terms *commodity* and *money* seem worthwhile, and it is provided in the appendix to this chapter.

FIVE CONCEPTS

Use-Value

The term "use-value" denotes a property and, derivatively, things that have the property, so that what *has* (a)[3] use-value *is* a use-value. The use-value of a thing is its power to satisfy, directly or indirectly, a human desire (see for example, Marx, 1972, p. 129). It satisfies a desire indirectly when it is used in the production or acquisition of another use-value. Otherwise, it satisfies a desire directly.

The use-value of an automobile is, *inter alia*, its power to transport people and, depending on the type of automobile, with a certain measure of speed and comfort. The desire to move with speed and comfort renders that power a use-value. The use-value of water is its power to quench thirst, to extinguish fire, and to otherwise service human desire.

It is false that all human beings desire the same things or that to the extent that they do they want the same services from them. But as long as there is at least one desire something is able to satisfy, that thing has a use-value.

Commodity

The term "commodity" denotes use-values by virtue of the status they sometimes assume. It is thus far comparable to the term "chairman," which denotes people by virtue of a status they sometimes assume. The application of chairman presupposes that social relations of a certain type obtain; so does the application of commodity. (The same is not true of use-value.)

Because "commodity" sometimes denotes status of use-values, a use-value that is at one time or in one respect a commodity may be a noncommodity in other circumstances. Under what conditions does a use-value assume commodity status? It does so when it is offered for or exchanged for another use-value or use-values in general; in other words, when it is either undergoing a market transaction or is "on the market."

Exchange-Value

Exchange-value is a property of use-values that possess commodity status.[4] The exchange-value of a commodity is its power of exchange against quantities of other commodities. It is measured by the number of commodities of any other kind for which it will exchange under equilibrium market conditions.[5] Thus, the exchange-value of a coat might be eight shirts, three hats, or ten pounds sterling.

According to Marx, the exchange-value of a commodity varies directly and uniformly with the quantity of labor-time required to produce the commodity under standard conditions of productivity, and inversely and uniformly with the quantity of labor-time standardly required to produce other commodities, and with no further circumstance. This is not a result of the definition of exchange-value, but of an additional Marxist thesis, which will be neither asserted nor denied in this chapter. That the thesis is not true by mere definition was recognized by Lenin, who wrote that "exchange-value is *first of all* the ratio, the proportion, in which a certain number of use-values of one kind can be exchanged for a certain number of use-values of another kind" (Lenin, 1967, p. 22, italics mine).

Just as that which has use-value is itself a use-value, so that which has exchange-value is an exchange-value.[6]

Money

We defined use-value as the power to satisfy, directly or indirectly, a human desire; and exchange-value as the power of exchanging against (other) commodities. But the power of exchanging against commodities serves indirectly to satisfy human desire, since it enables the acquisition of use-values. It follows that exchange-value is a species of use-value. (I shall nevertheless sometimes use "use-value" as an abbreviation for "use-value that is independent of exchange-value," in contexts where misunderstanding is unlikely.)

We now define *money* as a commodity which (1) has use-value only because it has exchange-value and (2) is generally acceptable to commodity exchangers. While money has use-value only because it has exchange-value, its exchange-value is *not* its only use-value; for it also has use-value that is entirely due to, but not part of, its exchange-value. A wealthy man may obtain prestige or political power by virtue of his wealth. Yet he need not literally buy these influential characteristics, since he need not transfer any money to get them. They are use-values he acquires by virtue of the exchange-value he has; but, unlike the power to acquire diamond cufflinks, the power to obtain influence is not part of the exchange-value he has.

Because its use-value depends entirely on its exchange-value, money bears a unique relation to desire. A man wanting a nonmonetary commodity, say an automobile, may want both a certain number of that commodity, say one or two, and a certain kind of that commodity, say a sportscar or a Rolls

Royce. But a person who desires money desires only an amount of it, and does not care what kind he gets. If he is in Scotland he will desire a Scottish pound exactly as much as he desires an English pound (Marx, 1953, pp. 872, 936). If he prefers the Scottish because of its design, then it is not in its quality as money, as vessel of exchange-value, that he prefers it. If his interest is in money as money, then he also does not care about the currency composition of his money, where it has one. He cares only about how much he has.[7]

Capital

Capital is a form of exchange-value. I shall introduce the concept by describing some varieties of market exchange.

An exchanger can offer either money (M) or a nonmonetary commodity (C). And he can take either M or C. One kind of exchange is barter, whose schematic representation[8] is:

$$C\text{-}C' \tag{1}$$

In (1), a person brings a C to market and returns with a C of another kind. It might be a pair of trousers that he exchanges for a bushel of wheat. He does not want the trousers, or he wants them less than the wheat, so he surrenders them in favor of the wheat.

In another kind of exchange, money appears, mediating the transaction:

$$C\text{-}M\text{-}C' \tag{2}$$

Here, the man exchanges the trousers for money, with which in turn he buys the wheat.

In a third kind of exchange, money functions as capital:

$$M\text{-}C\text{-}M' \tag{3}$$

In (3), a person acquires, say, trousers by paying money, and sells them for a larger sum of money than he paid. He seeks M', not because it differs in kind from M (for it does not), but because it exceeds M in quantity. Bad luck or commercial ineptitude may force him to accept an M' smaller than M, but a reduction of M is not the purpose of (3). A person wanting to diminish his stock of money will give or throw some of it away rather than engage in (3).[9]

In exchange-circuit (3), M is capital, because it is *exchange-value exchanged with a view to increasing the amount of exchange-value possessed by its owner*. When the aim is fullfilled, an accumulation of capital occurs. A merchant capitalist accumulates by buying goods and then selling them. Another way of accumulating capital is by lending it at interest.[10]

The capitalist need not by definition employ money, as opposed to a nonmonetary exchange-value. A person who lends ten cows on condition of receiving fifteen cows at the end of five years may be using the cows as interest-bearing capital.[11] A merchant might repeatedly exchange one nonmonetary commodity for another. If he does so because later commodities in the series have more exchange-value, then he acts as a capitalist, despite the fact that his transactions take the form of barter and may be represented as (1) repeating itself: $C\text{-}C'\text{-}C''\text{-}\ldots\text{-}C^n$. For functional reasons, capitalist dealing normally involves money. But capital is by definition a species not of money but of exchange-value.

A third way of accumulating capital is by exchanging M for a C which consists of the requisites of production: labor power (LP) and raw materials, tools, premises, etc., collectively known as means of production (MP), with a view to combining them in a productive process whose result, C', can be marketed for more than M. This operation may be schematized as follows:

$$M\text{-}C \quad {LP \atop MP} \ldots P \ldots C'\text{-}M' \tag{4}$$

" $\ldots P \ldots$ " signifies the fact that in this mode of accumulation—by contrast with (3)—the process of exchange is interrupted by a process of production in which C is consumed and C' is produced through its consumption.

Marx calls capital moving in exchange circuit (4) "industrial" capital, but it would be better to call it "employing" capital, since it is distinguished by the hiring of labor power and it appears in agriculture as well as industry. Society is capitalist when most of its production is inside circuit (4), and there is a class of hirers of labor power distinct from the class of laborers. The first provision does not entail the second, and we shall later have occasion to describe three social forms whose production is capitalistic, but which are not capitalist since they lack class division.[12]

How is capital accumulation possible? How do the various types of capitalists emerge with more exchange-value than they had initially?

The Marxist answer comes from the labor theory of value. All exchange-value is created in the productive process, none by the exchange of goods. Therefore, those who acquire exchange-value by exchanging commodities always do so at the expense of producers.

This thesis does not enter the definition of capital given previously. Bourgeois economists do not use that definition, but they could and still remain bourgeois. In particular, schema (4) is an uncontroversial representation of how an industrialist proceeds. The schema does not imply that it is the presence of *LP* in the circuit that brings about *M'* exceeding *M*. *The theses of the labor theory of value are not presupposed or entailed by any contentions offered in the remainder of this chapter.*

THE SUBJUGATION OF USE–VALUE BY EXCHANGE–VALUE

We now examine how exchange-value supplants use-value as the regulator of productive activity and, to a lesser extent, as the object of human desire. Using Marxian materials, I construct a sequence in the course of which there arises the pursuit of exchange-value as an independent aim and, later, the subordination of society to that pursuit. The degree of historical verisimilitude of the sequence does not affect the subsequent exposition of a distinctive contradiction of advanced capitalism. What does matter is that the last member of the sequence is real.

Market exchange does not occur without production, but production may proceed and products circulate without market exchange. Products go from producer to consumer without passing through the sphere of exchange when they move in accordance with customary rules (e.g., of gift), or in accordance with a distributive plan, either democratically adopted or imposed by a dictatorial authority.

Marx thought products circulated without market exchange in earliest history. The first instance of market exchange is trade between independent tribes. Trade first appears between, rather than within, tribes because it presupposes separate ownership on each side of the trading transaction. Separate ownership in turn presupposes a certain independence of the exchangers from one another. But the members of the tribe perceive themselves to be united with one another. They lack the requisite independence. They have it only collectively, vis-à-vis other tribes, so that if two tribes or members of two tribes meet, trade is possible. Those conducting the trading transaction will be agents of their respective tribes, not independent merchants.

Once trade between tribes develops, the principle of market exchange begins to penetrate the interior of the tribal community, and intratribal trade is inaugurated. Commerce is responsible for the dissolution of primitive solidarity (Marx, 1904, pp. 53-54; 1953, pp. 87, 628, 756, 904, 921; 1961, pp. 87-88, 351-352; 1962, p. 174).

At first, trade takes the form of barter. But the barter form restricts the volume and pace of commodity circulation. The scope of exchange is extended by the emergence of money as the medium of exchange and measure and store of value. Now, trade takes the form $C\text{-}M\text{-}C'$. The producer exchanges his product for money in order to purchase and then consume the product of another producer, who does likewise. Each sells in order to buy in order to consume. C and C' issue from production and end in consumption, and M only facilitates their passage between these termini. Production and exchange are oriented to consumption and therefore to use-value.

Nevertheless, in this consumption-grounded form of trade, exchange-value has achieved an independent manifestation in an object useless for consumption, which has no use-value apart from its exchange-value, to wit, M. The precondition of the merchant's entry is fulfilled.[13] His activity rationalizes and accelerates commodity circulation. It suits producers to sell C to and buy C' from the merchant. For producers, M remains a medium of exchange, but for the merchant it is capital. The circuit of his activity is M-C-M'—he buys in order to sell. The merchant uses exchange-value to increase exchange-value, though he recurrently transforms M into what has use-value for consumption (C) in order to increase it. *Qua* merchant, he neither produces nor consumes the C he handles, and its qualities are of no interest to him—he cares only about its exchange-value.

Initially, the merchant who uses M as capital lacks what I shall call a *capitalist mentality*. The merchant does not personify capital, for his final object is to cash M' in for consumables, thus benefiting in use-value from the difference between M and M'. But there is a natural progression from this merchant to another merchant who is a living embodiment of M-C-M' and who aims to increase his stock of exchange-value without limit, or at least beyond the limits set by his consumption demands. The merchant who thus personifies the capitalist principle is likely to grow larger and stronger than the modest merchant who does not.

Thus, barter leads by easy steps to the *capitalist principle*—the use of exchange-value to increase exchange-value. The capitalist principle engenders the *capitalist mentality*—the quest for exchange-value which is not controlled by a desire for use-value. The reality of the principle and the mentality is undeniable,[14] though the story just given of their genesis is highly stylized.

In general, the principle and the mentality promote one another, though they need not go together. A man who handles the funds of an orphanage in an attempt to increase them for the sake of the children's welfare, employs the principle but lacks the mentality. He may well drive harder bargains than the mentally capitalist trader, who may be restrained by the fact that his trading lacks underlying moral justification.

Conversely, a man who does not use exchange-value to increase exchange-value may have a capitalist mentality. A miserly craftsman who transforms his earnings into a hoard of gold operates noncapitalistically but possesses a capitalist mentality. A modern worker has something of a capitalist mentality if his furniture pleases him because it costs a lot, and not just because he enjoys its comforts.

Both principle and mentality antedate capitalist society. In capitalist society, all the elements of the productive process have become objects of purchase and sale. The principal capitalist is no longer the merchant but the industrialist, whose enterprise, unlike the merchant's, essentially involves the employment of labor power. (This differentiation does not depend on the labor theory of value, for it does not imply that labor is the source of the industrialist's profit.)

As society develops toward capitalism, larger and larger portions of the productive process fall subject to the capitalist principle. Capitalism is preceded by a succession of mercantile conquests. At first, the merchant disposes only of the surplus product of producers. As the division of labor deepens (partly as a result of new market opportunities created by mercantile enterprise), the merchant begins to handle the entire product. Control of the producer's raw materials is the next result, followed by control of the tools, which the producer must rent from the merchant. Finally, the producer's labor power becomes a commodity, and the capitalist becomes an industrialist.[15] The formation of the labor market completes the subordination of production to exchange. Now, consumable use-values are produced only because they have exchange-value, and only if the industrialist expects to expand exchange-value through their production and sale. Concrete wealth, an ensemble of qualitatively different use-values, cedes precedence to abstract wealth, a quantum of featureless exchange-value. For "the immediate purpose of capitalist production is not 'the possession of . . . goods,' but the appropriation of value, of money, of abstract wealth" (Marx, 1969, p. 503).

A DISTINCTIVE CONTRADICTION
OF ADVANCED CAPITALISM

The pursuit of abstract wealth proceeds apace in the capitalism of our own time. Whatever other goals a corporation has, it must, on pain of bankruptcy, obey the imperative *expand the exchange-value at your disposal*. This imperative holds whether firms aim at profit or growth, for they are different modes of increasing exchange-value; and a firm must aim at one or the other. It also holds whether or not managerialist theses are true: whoever wields ultimate corporate power is constrained to favor decisions that enlarge the difference between M and M'.

It is a paradox that in just this society, consumption, whose demands are essentially finite according to a tradition descending from antiquity,[16] eventually knows no bounds. I shall argue that consumer demand becomes bloated when and because production does not have consumption as its controlling goal, when "the product is from the outset subsumed under capital, and comes into being only for the purpose of increasing that capital" (Marx, 1968, p. 401). This paradox is not what I mean by "a distinctive contradiction of advanced capitalism," for that is a matter of productive forces and production relations. I first explain how advanced capitalism produces the paradoxical situation, and then reveal the contradiction associated with it.

Capitalist society is responsible for technological power on an unprecedented scale, progressing at an unprecedented rate. This is because the competitive position of its industrial decision makers compels them to increase the productivity of production processes. The compulsion does not lapse when capitalism reaches its misnamed "monopoly stage," for competition persists in pertinent respects. Since total consumer spending power is finite, heterogeneous products of monopolized industries compete against one another for buyers. There is also competition for shareholders, for loan capital, for skilled labor, etc.

Improvement in productivity is a condition of survival and success in the multidimensional competition that characterizes capitalism in *all* of its stages. "It is therefore the economic tendency of capital which teaches humanity to husband its strength and to achieve its productive aim with the least possible expenditure of means" (Marx, 1969, p. 548).

Now, improvements in productivity, whether labor-saving or capital-saving,[17] are open to two uses. One way of exploiting enhanced productivity is to reduce toil and extend leisure, while maintaining constant output. Alternatively, output may be increased while labor stays the same. It is also possible to achieve a measure of both *desiderata*.

"Leisure" is used broadly here, in rough synonymy with "freedom from unappealing activity," while "toil" abbreviates "unappealing activity." Leisure means that a person's time and energy are not spent in the service of goals he would prefer fulfilled without such expenditure. One toils to the extent that the motivation of his activity is remuneration or other external reward. It follows that leisure time can be filled strenuously. It also follows that amelioration of working conditions counts as expanding leisure.

The economic distinction between job time and time off coincides imperfectly with the distinction here envisaged between toil and freedom from it. Some "gainful employment" is enjoyable, and some time off is spent toilsomely. But the distinctions are sufficiently coextensive for the purposes of my argument. It is enough that for most people most of the time earning a living is not a joy. Most people are so situated that they would benefit not only from more goods and services but also from reduced working hours. It is clear that advances in productivity enable gains in either direction, typically at the expense of gains in the other direction.

Now, capitalism inherently tends to promote just one of the options—output expansion—since the other, toil reduction, threatens a sacrifice of the profit associated with increased output and sales, and hence a loss of competitive strength.[18] There has indeed been a titanic growth of output and a negligible reduction of labor expenditure in the history of capitalism. That the reduction in the working day has been negligible by comparison with the volume of output expansion is beyond controversy, whatever date is chosen as base line. But it is arguable that the reduction has also been fairly small in absolute terms, if sophisticated but defensible criteria of the amount of time men spend supporting themselves are adopted. Meriting consideration here are such activities as traveling to work, shopping experienced as a nuisance, and other activities in themselves unattractive but performed as a means of fulfilling consumption purposes.[19] In sheer hours of work per year, the modern American worker is not obviously better off than the European peasant of the Middle Ages, many of whose days were idle because the weather and the observance of the Christian calendar made them so. Nor has there been much lessening of total working hours since 1920, if everything relevant—notably overtime work—is taken into account. There has, of course, been an impressive decline in labor time since the middle of the nineteenth century, but capitalism as a system need not be thanked for effecting it, since it was capitalism that stretched out the working day in the first place. In any case, even that decline is nothing compared with the accompanying increase in output; and the bias I attribute to capitalism is sufficiently evidenced by the relative position.

Output expansion takes different forms. If the market for the good whose production has improved is expandible, output expansion may take the direct form of more products of the same kind. Otherwise, and especially if the market in question is more or less saturated, output expands elsewhere, as newly available funds find their way into another line of industry, via diversification, takeovers, deposit in financial institutions, etc. This does not always occur immediately or smoothly, but eventually it occurs. Typically, jobs are destroyed and created in the process.

As long as the capitalist principle prevails in competitive conditions, the output-increasing option will tend to be selected and implemented one way or another. Whether or not capitalists have capitalist mentalities, it is imperative for them to continue accumulating exchange-value, and thus to expand output. But it is inconceivable that the capitalist principle should prevail while the mentality is wholly absent, and the mentality fortifies and adds to the effect of the principle itself.

Now, the consequence of the increasing output, which capitalism necessarily favors, is increasing consumption. Hence, the boundless pursuit of consumption goods is a result of a productive process oriented to exchange- rather than consumption-values. It is the Rockefellers who ensure that the Smiths need to keep up with the Joneses.[20]

The productive forces of advanced capitalism create an unparalleled opportunity of lifting the curse of Adam and liberating men from toil, but the production relations of capitalist ownership prevent the opportunity from being seized. The economic form most able to relieve toil is least willing to do so (Marx, 1968, pp. 235–236). In earlier periods of capitalist history, the bias toward output gave capitalism a progressive historical role. Capitalism is an incomparable engine for producing material wealth in conditions of scarcity, and that is its "historical justification (Marx, 1969, p. 405). But as scarcity recedes, the same bias renders the system reactionary—it cannot realize the possibilities of liberation it creates. It excludes liberation by feverish product innovation, huge investments in sales and advertising, and contrived obsolescence. It brings society to the threshold of abundance and then locks the door. For the promise of abundance is not a maximum of goods but a sufficiency produced by a minimum of unpleasant exertion.

The dynamic of advanced capitalism arguably infringes on the limits of human nature. It certainly violates the limits of physical nature. The disaffection of part of the young middle class with its forms of work and consumption may anticipate in miniature the response of human nature to advanced capitalism. The pollution/resources crisis, present or future, is the unequivocal answer it gets from the elements.

The permanent contradictions of capitalism discussed in Marxist economic literature (or, if you prefer, the difficulties known to Keynsians) incline the system to an underemployment of resources. The contradiction distinctive of advanced capitalism generates their overemployment. Since the permanent contradictions are not cancelled by the emergence of the distinctive contradiction, the result is grotesque overemployment in some directions and injurious underemployment in others.

The consequences of the distinctive contradiction are familiar. They are emphasized by critics of "economic growth"[21] such as Mishan and Galbraith. This chapter is an attempt along Marxist lines to explain what they deplore. Mishan (1967) sees what he calls "growthmania" as a property of advanced industrial society, as such, or of the "growthmen" whose ideology governs it. He largely ignores the capitalist structuring of industry. A small section of his Costs of Economic Growth is entitled "Profit-Propelled Growth." Yet, the evils he identifies in the rest of the book are also attributable to profit-propulsion, to the enclosure of production within circuit (4). Mishan grounds the evils in the mania for growth, a syndrome he does not attempt to explain. I regard this mania as the natural reflection in consciousness of practical adherence to the capitalist principle.

Galbraith's purview is larger than Mishan's. He does not refer the bias in favor of output to growthmania. He believes it is not "the images of ideology" but "the imperatives of technology and organization" that "determine the shape of economic society" (Galbraith, 1967, p. 18). Advanced technology generates new power relationships, which in turn establish the primacy of production. In particular, technology shifts power to the highly trained men who operate it. The "technostructure" of salaried engineers, economists, market analysts, personnel experts, etc., wrests control from entrepreneurs, shareholders, and bankers. Let us accept that there is this transfer of power. The rest of the argument is as follows. Since "the technostructure is principally concerned with the manufacture of goods and with the companion management and development of demand for these goods" (Galbraith, 1967, p. 169), a strong bias in favor of more goods is assured.

But once we recall that advanced technology may also be used to reduce toil, Galbraith's account is seen to be question-begging. Grant that sophisticated technology confers power on technical experts. It does not follow, unless the need to make profit—of secondary import for Galbraith—is introduced, that they will favor output, not leisure. One elaboration of this point follows.

Members of the technostructure have skills of two kinds. Some (for example, those of the sales force) are especially suited to promoting consumption, but others (for example, those of production engineers) could also be used to extend leisure.[22] The fact that technology gives authority to men with technical knowledge explains neither the demand for the first set of skills nor the use to which the second set is put. It also does not explain why the skilled obtain advancement and kudos by delivering the goods rather than the free time. What explains these phenomena is the extratechnological fact that this technology appears within a capitalist economic structure. The supposed circumstance that production is in the grip of unchallengeable experts leaves the choice between· output and leisure open. It is closed by the imperative of capital accumulation alone.

The great fault in Galbraith's position is that he relates the output emphasis to the modern firm's *transcendence* of market constraints, whereas its source is in the *persistence* of those constraints. The humble truth—that even the huge corporation must earn money—receives more attention in another Galbraith book (1973), in the course of his discussion of the "protective purposes" of the technostructure.[23] He also momentarily acknowledges that public enterprise need not so protect itself.[24] And at one point he recognizes that the ideology of output preceded the technostructure's advent.[25] A proper development of these submerged truths sustains the conclusion that output mania belongs to capitalism as such, whatever variation the technostructure plays on the theme.

THE ARGUMENT REVIEWED

Key positions in the argument are:

1. Capitalist competition promotes increases in productivity, which enable both expansion of output and reduction of toil.
2. Capitalist competition engenders a bias in favor of expanding output as against reducing toil.
3. Both more output and less toil benefit people. The current endowment of goods and leisure will determine which use of productivity improvement is currently preferable. It will sometimes be rational to prefer the leisure-increasing use.
4. Because capitalism always favors expanding output, it sometimes behaves irrationally.
5. For some value of "very high" and some value of "substantial," capitalism behaves irrationally when consumption is very high and the working day is substantial.
6. Consumption is relevantly high and the working day is relevantly substantial in the United States now. Hence, American capitalism now behaves irrationally.

Different kinds of claims are lodged here. Statements one and two depend on elementary economic reasoning. To prevail in competition, capitalist firms must be favorably disposed to technical innovation and to an output-expanding use of that innovation. Statements one and two require no special premises about human nature. They follow from what is true of the mere structure of capitalist economies.

Statement three does say something about the sources of human welfare, but nothing controversial.

Statement four follows from statements two and three.

Statement five identifies a type of case that illustrates the truth of statement four.

Statement six claims that American capitalism is a concrete example of what five describes. Statement six is a *judgment*, which I have not defended. But it is not a judgment that may be dismissed as merely eccentric.

To recapitulate, I am arguing that even if and when it becomes possible and desirable to reduce unwanted activity, capitalism continues to promote consumption instead and therefore functions irrationally. The structure of the economy militates against optimal use of its productive capacity. It is undeniable that capitalist relations of production possess an output-expanding bias. So the only way of denying that they are potentially irrational in the stated respect is to assert that labor is so enjoyable (or not so unenjoyable) and resources are so plentiful and the satisfaction to be had from goods and services is so limitless that no matter how much is being consumed it remains desirable to consume more instead of expanding freedom from labor. And that is a pretty tall assertion.

The heart of the matter is that capitalist firms are so placed that they will assess productive activity only in terms of its extrinsic value. Its impact on the producer is irrelevant, except where that has extrinsic effects (improved working conditions sometimes' raise output, but the point is of minor significance here). For a long time, the benefits of this tilted decision making outweigh the sacrifice exacted in labor. But when output is of a very high order, and it remains true that most people devote most of their energy to doing what they would rather not do, then to persist in favor of further output at the expense of relief from undesired work is irrational.

The reader may have noticed that no specifically Marxian concepts were employed in the review of the argument. And some participants at the conference maintained that the economic part of the argument could be formulated in neoclassical terms, with no loss in persuasive power.

I am happy to agree with them. The main economic argument—the argument for statement two—is an easy deduction from entirely familiar facts about competition. Neoclassical economics would be defective indeed if it were unable to present that argument.

So the question arises, why did I use Marxian terminology, which I took such pains to explain?

The basis of the argument is the incontrovertible proposition that, *in Marxian terms*, capitalist production is production for exchange-value. Acceptance of the proposition involves no commitment to the contested labor theory of value. Once its meaning is explained, its truth is obvious. And the truth can then be expressed in non-Marxian terms. Alfred P. Sloan recognized the truth when he said it was the business of the automobile industry to make money, not cars.

The result I go on to derive—that capitalism will favor output at the expense of freedom from toil—follows almost immediately. *But where does neoclassical economics devote attention to it?* It is not, after all, an uninteresting result. Its neglect by established economics needs to be explained, because, though trivial intellectually, it is momentous for our view of capitalism. And that is the explanation. It is neglected *because of* its importance for our view of capitalism.

Neoclassical economists proceed as though the governing goal of the capitalist system and its constituent firms is the production of goods and services. In fact it is not.[26] As Sloan acknowledged, the production of goods and services fulfills a more basic *desideratum* of the system. To requote Marx: "The immediate purpose of capitalist production is not 'the possession of . . . goods,' but the appropriation of value, of money, of abstract wealth" (Marx, 1969, p. 503). The technical apparatus used by academic economists does not prevent them from giving rigorous and elegant formulation to that point. Their capitalist ideology intervenes to obscure the point and its consequences.

Marx complained that bourgeois economists were inclined to fudge the distinction between capitalist production and production in general; it was a good way of preventing the system from being seen as one alternative among others. The purpose of production in general—satisfaction of human desires—will also look like the purpose of capitalist production when its capitalist character is not emphasized.

Official economics still fails to acknowledge fully the *specificity* of capitalism.[27] An effective way of revealing what is special about capitalism is by means of the concepts elaborated at the beginning of this paper. The results that then follow belong to the Marxian tradition, very much in contrast with the bourgeois. That justifies the Marxian framework of my presentation.

IS CAPITALISM A NECESSARY CONDITION OF THE DISTINCTIVE CONTRADICTION?

The argument shows only that capitalism is a sufficient condition of the distinctive contradiction. Is it also a necessary condition? Do other economic forms generate the same irrationality? Would the overthrow of capitalism ensure escape from it?

Capitalism was defined on pages 112–113 as a society whose production is governed by the capitalist principle and that exhibits a division between a capitalist and a laboring class. But capitalism's preference for output depends on the first feature alone. We may envisage class-united societies whose production follows the capitalist principle. I will depict three such societies before considering one whose production is not subject to the principle.

All three may be called *egalitarian market societies.* In each, competition induces a tendency to output expansion, but to only two of them may we also ascribe movement toward the distinctive contradiction. None has occurred in history, and none represents a viable alternative for the future.

The first society is a variant of what Marx called "simple commodity production," a market economy of self-employed producers who hire no labor. Given sufficient competition, each producer will be motivated to raise his productivity, lest competitors who do so drive him out of the market by outselling him. (Productivity is improved, for example, by use of superior producer goods sold by innovating blacksmiths.) What is more, he will be inclined to exploit increased productivity for output expansion, since only by the extra sales thereby gained will he be able to finance further productivity improvements. But simple commodity production is incompatible with really advanced technology—which socializes labor—and also with really high output. Its tendency to promote "economic growth" would lead to its self-destruction and replacement by capitalism, not to the distinctive contradiction.

The second type, supposedly attempted in Yugoslavia, is a set of firms, each of which is wholly owned by its employees, who share fairly equally the firm's income. If this structure could be sustained, there would be movement toward the contradiction, though the bias in favor of output would receive less ideological and political support than in capitalism proper, since no powerful class would benefit differentially from it. Transcendence of the capitalist principle would not discriminate against the interests of a dominant minority.

The last case—call it "people's capitalism"—differs from the second in that share ownership is not restricted to the employee's firm. In addition—to keep the system egalitarian—there is a duty of all to work and an income ceiling so that distinct classes are not precipitated. If these stringent conditions were realized, there would be movement toward the contradiction. Once again, however, no special section of society would benefit from it.

The last two models are instructive—they show that it is not in virtue of its inequality that capitalism slides toward the contradiction. Those systems have never occurred, and they are not reasonable options now, for they are too unstable. In the course of an inevitably "uneven development," some firms would outpace others, which would foster a division into employers and employees. The tendency could be arrested by a complex insurance scheme, but it would have to be so comprehensive that the economy would lose its market character. The envisaged forms are counterexamples to the proposition that capitalism is in principle a necessary condition of the contradiction, but their unviability confirms the claim that it is a necessary condition *in practice*.

Turn now to a nonmarket society, with centralized production under a common authority, democratic (as in genuine socialism) or otherwise. This will not generate the contradiction. For the decision makers are free, *as far as systematic economic constraints are concerned*, to choose between expanding output and reducing labor, when there is progress in productivity. A dictatorship might seek to maintain constant labor, even in conditions of affluence, fearing that people with free time would be more difficult to rule. But this would be choice, not, as with capitalism, a dictate of the impersonal logic of the economic system. But the latter is required to impute contradiction, which by definition holds between productive forces and production relations, not between productive forces and the particular wills of particular men. We are looking for irrationality in the nature of the economic system itself.

I therefore conclude that the capitalist principle alone induces an economic-systemic bias toward output expansion, and that, if we consider feasible economies only, then capitalism is not just a sufficient but also a necessary condition of the emergence of the distinctive contradiction.

Even if accurate within its own terms, the argument may seem disappointing. For it is conceded that a noncapitalist regime may in fact sustain a drive for more and more output, the insistence being merely that the economy over which it presides does not engender that drive. And indeed there is good reason to think that the Soviet Union's leadership, bent on "overtaking capitalism," will continue to stress production before all else even when that emphasis ceases to be defensible.[28] I once remarked, in conversation with Soviet academicians, that whereas an American manager is motivated to conceal pollution caused by his plant, a Soviet manager can report it and request subventions to counteract it. One sociologist replied: "You are naive. If he publicizes it, he will be replaced by a manager who is more discreet."

For all that, the distinction between a policy choice and the natural result of the normal functioning of an economic system retains intellectual and practical importance. There are surface resemblances between the maladies of the Soviet Union and the United States; but different diagnoses apply, and different remedies are required. Political change in the Soviet Union could lead to altered priorities, with no dramatic disruption of its economic system. In America the problem is different. It is hard to conceive of governmental measures that could arrest the impulsion toward output expansion without striking at the heart of the capitalist system itself. It is not so easy to see how America will be able to deal effectively with pollution, which is just one side of the problem. Capitalist enterprise does not thrive hedged around by regulations and directives, even supposing their passage and enforcement is politically feasible in the face of corporate power.

It would be pointless to consider in the space of a few sentences which society is more likely to change course.

AN OBJECTION

Someone might say, "You have proved at most that capitalism *tends* to select output expansion. It does not follow that if it actually expands output, then this is adequately explained by the bias you have identified. There are other tendencies attributable to capitalism on similar grounds—the need to accumulate capital—that are completely unfulfilled. One is the tendency of firms not to raise their workers' wages. This tendency is never eliminated, but its effect is nullified by countervailing trade union power. Why does that same power not check the propensity toward output? Why do unions generally press for more income rather than less labor? If the system's bias harms their members' interests, why do they cooperate with it? When the contradiction looms, why does union policy not change? If the United States has crossed the border into contradiction, why is union policy what it is?"

Note that the objection is *not* that output expansion is favored not by the system but only by the aims the population wants the system to accomplish. That claim cannot stand, since the system demonstrably possesses an output-expanding bias. But the presence of that tendency does not suffice to explain its realization. That lesser claim is the basis of the objection.

I shall meet the objection by appealing to premises that are minimally controversial. It is easily met on the Marcusean premise that much of what is consumed gives no real satisfaction but people cherish it because they are dupes of advertising and ideology. Although I believe a reduced version of that thesis is capable of defense, the envisaged opponent does not, and I am unable to provide the defense here.

So let us suppose, against Marcuse and his ilk, that by and large the given consumer goods are desirable, that desire for them is in some relevant sense awakened, not contrived, by advertising and affiliated processes, and that the satisfaction they afford is genuine. On the other side, the opponent must concede that plenty of labor is not desired. If God gave workers *gratis* the pay they now get, and granted them freedom to choose whether or not to work at their jobs, for as long as they pleased, without remuneration, then there would result a very substantial decline in laboring activity.

What advertising may be said to do, on the most generous account, is to draw attention to and emphasize what we suppose are the independently desirable qualities of the products it displays. This is balanced by no similar campaign stressing the goods of leisure. No ads say: "When *your* union negotiates, make it go for shorter hours, not more pay. Electric carving knives are fine, but nothing beats freedom." There are no "leisure ads," because firms have no interest in financing them. There is, of course, advertisement of leisure products, such as snowmobiles. But rising income is required to procure them. One can imagine someone saying, in an extreme case, "I am taking a weekend job to maintain the payments on the snowmobile I use on weekends."

Thus, labor acquiescence in the bias is itself traceable to the bias—workers are influenced by its operation in the emphases promoted by the media.[29]

Finally, a reply to those who use their leisure time arguing that if people had lots of it they would not know how to use it. No well-confirmed propositions about human nature support this arrogant pessimism. It is, moreover, predictable that a society rigged up to maximize output will fail to develop the theory and practice of leisure. And indeed this further manifestation of the output bias adds to the explanation of general acquiescence in it. Many workers may prefer *well-filled* leisure to more goods, but they go for goods out of anxiety that they would not know how to fill their leisure well. It does not follow that their preference for leisure is mistaken.

THE DISTINCTIVE CONTRADICTION AND MAX WEBER

We have seen that in capitalist *practice* it is a mistake to reduce labor time when output can be raised instead. There is no room to expose how pervasive this emphasis is in bourgeois *ideology*. It operates as an unstated premise in much academic analysis. I limit myself to one instructive example.

Max Weber did not welcome every aspect of capitalist civilization. But he did turn its pathetic preference for output into a canon of rationality (Weber, 1961):

> At the beginning of all ethics and the economic relations which result, is traditionalism, the sanctity of tradition, the exclusive reliance upon such trade and industry as have come down from the fathers. This traditionalism survives far down into the present; only a human lifetime in the past it was futile to double the wages of an agricultural laborer in Silesia who mowed a certain tract of land on a contract, in the hope of inducing him to increase his exertions. He would simply have reduced by half the work expended because with this half he would have been able to earn [as much as before]. This general incapacity and indisposition to depart from the beaten paths is the motive for the maintenance of tradition. (pp. 260-261)

Weber regarded the peasant's response as other than rational, for he tendentiously contrasted "traditional" and "rational" behavior. Yet Weber failed to show that the peasant reacted traditionally and, hence, from Weber's viewpoint, nonrationally. For the peasant did not continue in his traditional ways. He began to work much less than he had before, and thus to forsake tradition at least as much as if he had begun to work harder at twice the old wage rate. Only a fixation on material goods as against freedom from toil could incline one to think otherwise. Indeed, the peasant's choice was probably rational. He could not be certain what increase in consumption welfare would attend the rise in money income—clearly, it would not have doubled as a result. Reasonable conjectures regarding the marginal utility of goods and the marginal disutility of labor suggest that in opting for labor reduction he won a more substantial benefit.

APPENDIX: FURTHER REMARKS
ON "COMMODITY" AND "MONEY"

FURTHER REMARKS ON COMMODITIES

I said that a use-value that is at one time or in one respect a commodity may be a noncommodity in other circumstances. Let me now illustrate this point.

If a farmer produces a gallon of milk for his family's consumption and does not sell or barter it, the milk is not a commodity. But if someone had intercepted the milk and brought it to market, the milk would then be a commodity. Again, if a person eats a bun bought at a bakery, he is not, strictly speaking, eating a commodity, since the bun ceases to be one when it reaches its final purchaser. It drops out of the sphere of exchange into the sphere of consumption and is no longer on the market.

The bun example shows how commodity status may attach to a use-value at one time but not another. An example of a use-value that is a commodity in one respect but not in another is a house that is both occupied and for sale. It is at once in the sphere of consumption and the sphere of exchange.

I have laid down strict criteria of commodity status, in accordance with Marx's instruction that a use-value "is a commodity in the strict sense of the word only within the framework of circulation" (Marx, 1972, pages 284–290). Marx practices this strict use when he denies that the seamstress whom the capitalist retains to produce his wife's dresses produces commodities, since the dresses are neither bought nor sold (Marx, 1968, p. 159, cf. pp. 164–165). But he often relaxes the restrictions and uses the term to denote any product that is exchanged at some point in its history, referring to it as a commodity even while it is in the production or consumption spheres; and he sometimes uses the term more broadly still, to denote any product in a market economy (see, for example, Marx, 1969, page 64). A liberal use is warranted by the fact that, in a market economy, almost any use-value is such that its owner, even if he has no intention of parting with it, would exchange it for another use-value if the terms are sufficiently attractive. In this limited sense, virtually all products in an exchange economy are at all times on the market.

FURTHER REMARKS ON MONEY

I defined money as the commodity that (a) has use-value only because it has exchange-value and (b) is generally acceptable to commodity exchangers.

Feature (A)

All commodities have use-value by virtue of having exchange-value, in addition to the use-value they have which is realized in consumption. (Consumption includes productive consumption, in which one use-value is used to produce another.) But money has use-values *only* by virtue of having exchange-value.

The functions commonly prescribed as definitive of money attach to it because the fact that money lacks use-value, aside from its exchange-value, makes it good at performing these functions. Money serves as medium of exchange, measure of value, means of payment, etc. But it is a mistake to *define* it by reference to these services, as opposed to the properties that make it supremely eligible to fulfill them.

Feature (B)

This provision implies that whether a commodity is money is a matter of degree, since acceptability is a matter of degree. By demanding *general* acceptability, I exclude such paper claims as stocks, certificates, bonds, railway tickets, etc. These and similar nonmonetary documents have no use-value apart from their exchange-value and they discharge some of the functions of money, but within restricted spheres of circulation.

I said that money-seekers will be indifferent to the kind of money they get (see page 111). Yet, some money is certainly "better" than others. American dollars, for example, are generally more desirable than Hungarian forints, because dollars are more widely accepted, which means [recall feature (b)] that they are money to a greater extent. Their superiority is thus no embarrassment to the position developed here.

The definition enables a distinction between money and what is used as money. Nonmoney is used as money when it fulfills functions of money but lacks one or both of money's defining properties. The items (stocks, certificates, bonds, and railway tickets) mentioned previously lack the second property. Certain primitive media of exchange (such as wheat and cattle) lack the first property. They occur in the sphere of consumption as well as in the sphere of exchange. Finally, any commodity can, at times, perform some of money's functions, even if it lacks both of the defining properties.

The definition has a certain peculiarity. Nothing in the world satisfies it completely, since nothing real is capable of monetary use only. Coins can pry open tins of tobacco and notes can feather a bed. But the exchange-value of coins and notes will normally exceed that of nonmonetary objects that perform similar consumption services only. It would be pointless to spend a penny or more on a tin opener that is no better than a penny at the job, does no other job better, and is not prettier. In general, money will be worth more than a cognate nonmonetary material object, for otherwise it will be taken out of circulation.

Because coins and notes so predominantly owe their use-value to their exchange-value, it is wiser to pretend that they satisfy the definition than to adopt a more involved definition that would accommodate the extra use-value they have. It is in spite of the fact that coins and notes are money that they have these residual use-values.

The residual utility—and disutility—of money also makes it necessary to modify the claim (see page 111) that currency composition is unimportant. It is of course true that 100 pennies are for most purposes less convenient than a one dollar bill. But such facts impose only very minor qualifications on what was said.

Finally, a word about the use of coins as tokens. This is not a monetary use. The authority (running a subway system, or in charge of parking meters) confers nonmonetary use-value on a coin by so designing a machine that the coin will make it work. Here, money as money buys money as nonmonetary use-value via a deftly arranged "short circuit" in the process of exchange. Currency preferences will, of course result, and a person might give more than ten pennies for a much needed dime, but these phenomena are not serious counterexamples to any important claims.

NOTES

1. I shall defend elsewhere the propriety of calling the irrationality I ascribe to advanced capitalism a "contradiction" in the sense of the quoted passage. A defense is needed, since I stress inhibitions on the *use* of productive forces, not primarily on their *development*. But whether I am entitled to the term "contradiction" is irrelevant to the strength of my argument, except for those who take conformity with Marx as a necessary condition of truth. Persons indifferent to that issue may read "systematic irrationality" for "contradiction."

2. These phenomena condition the mode of incidence and the degree of importance of the contradiction. In this chapter, I explain what the contradiction is. I do not discuss its relevance to political practice, which is considerable.

3. I parenthesize the indefinite article because wherever power is attributed, *a* power is attributed, and vice versa. Since (a) use-value is (a) power, the grammar is similar. Thus, Marx uses the term with and without the article, in the manner indicated.

4. Whether a use-value that is not on the market has exchange-value, as opposed to potential exchange-value, depends on how liberally the term *commodity* is used. See the appendix to this chapter, pp. 130–133.

5. These last two sentences are valid only on the conceptual level of Volume 1 of *Capital* (Marx, 1961). They need to be qualified to cater for deviations of price from exchange-value discussed in Volumes 2 and 3 (Marx, 1962, 1969). These deviations occur under equilibrium conditions. They are due, not to short-term movements of supply and demand, but to such permanent circumstances as commercial profit, divergent organic composition of capital, and rent. Since no commitment to Marx's *theory* of value is made in this paper, the simplification introduced in the text may stand.

6. I do not introduce the further concept, value *simpliciter*, here. It requires defense, and it is not needed for the purposes of this paper.

7. Real and apparent counterexamples to the claims of this section on money are dealt with in the appendix to this chapter, pp. 130–133.

8. I use Marx's code here, with one amendment: "*C*" stands for a nonmonetary commodity, and "*M*" for a sum of money. The prime sign indicates that the "*C*" or "*M*" to its left is different from the preceding "*C*" or "*M*" in the given exchange circuit. The hyphen is to be read "is exchanged for."

It is my use of the prime sign that differs from Marx's. His use of it reflects his theory of value, which is not espoused in this paper.

9. M' may by design be less than M if, for example, C is used by a retailer as a loss leader, or C is used in consumption before resale but without being materially changed. We can ignore such cases.

Rationality excludes exchanges of the forms $M\text{-}M'$ and $M\text{-}M$. Putative counterexamples depend on the residual use-values of money (e.g., paying a dime for a penny because a dime is too thin to pry open a tin) or on the use of coins as tokens or on the fact that different currencies may be money to different extents or in different spheres of circulation. See the appendix to this chapter, pp. 130–133.

10. $M(t)\text{-}M'$ $(t + n)$ serves to depict the circuit of interest-bearing capital, the parenthesized expressions denoting times when the money is transferred.

11. See Marx (1953, pp. 67, 884–885) for his acknowledgment that capital is possible without money.

12. See p. 125 in text.

13. Not in a logical sense, but effectively. It is difficult to operate as a merchant in the absence of a monetary medium of exchange.

14. Though the extent to which the mentality is present in an individual or a society is extremely difficult to judge.

15. This was the sequence in the textile industry, as Marx tells the story.

16. Aristotle, developing an idea of Plato's, contrasted trade that services the consumption needs of a household, whose circuit is $C\text{-}M\text{-}C'$, and "retail trade" $(M\text{-}C\text{-}M')$, whose aim is the accumulation of currency. He endorsed the first and condemned the second as a perversion of it. There is a natural term to the accumulation of Cs, but the virtues of order and limit are violated by the search for M, which is by nature endless. This criticism of the Sysyphan character of mercantile enterprise is often heard in Western intellectual history. Hume derided the merchant who knew "no such pleasure as that of seeing the daily increase of his fortune," and similar disdain informed much of the nineteenth century socialist and conservative (e.g., Carlyle) response to capitalism. The recommended alternative was not asceticism—at root, the merchant exhibits that—but enjoyment of use-value, the desire for which was supposed to be satiable. For further information, see Marx (1953, pp. 928–929; 1961, p. 588; 1968, pp. 174, 282–283, 302, 367, 374).

17. I here use "capital" in a non-Marxist sense. In Marx's language, capital-saving is "cheapening of the elements of constant capital" (Marx, 1962, p. 230). Capital-saving poses problems for the thesis of the falling rate of profit; but it does not threaten the present argument, since it clearly enables labor-reduction with constant output.

18. Marx never explicitly made this point, but passages may be cited in proof of its broadly Marxian pedigree. See Marx, (1953, pp. 589, 595–600; 1968, pp. 223, 226–228; 1969, p. 468). For a fascinating early case of the bias of capitalism, see Ashton (1945, p. 65).

19. Also needing attention, in more than just a footnote, is the complicated effect capitalism has on the amount of labor performed by women. To *some* extent, their leisure is increased because of the output bias, which causes a proliferation of devices that reduce domestic labor. On the other hand, the devices also encourage women to join the remunerated labor force, so their total effect is not easy to judge.

According to Galbraith (1973), the net result of introducing more and more goods into the home is to make housewives hard-pressed managers of consumption, so that "the menial role of the woman becomes more arduous the higher the family income." (p. 32) Galbraith is evidently no connoisseur of low-income family life, but there may be something—much less than he thinks—in what he says.

20. For a case in which the "conspiracy" to effect this result may be described without inverted commas, see Sklar (1969) which reports the concerted plan to stimulate consumption conceived under the aegis of the Hoover administration.

Note that I do not maintain that the Smiths are interested only in the use-value of commodities. Under capitalism, noncapitalists find exchange-value appealing, and like the fact that what they have is expensive, quite apart from enjoying the services it provides. See text, p. 115.

21. I use scare quotes because the reservations are really about certain criteria of economic growth. In calling what they oppose "economic growth," the critics make a gratuitous concession.

22. Skill individuation is a hazardous business, and the illustrations given could be challenged; but rigorous demarcation is not required for the argument offered here.

23. See Galbraith (1973, chap. 10). We are nevertheless told that "the power of the technostructure, so long as the firm is making money, is plenary" (p. 40). Even if this is true, the qualification is of momentous import. The need to make money by itself induces an output bias and explains why we have the kind of technostructure we do.

24. "A public organization will not need a minimal level of earnings to protect its autonomy" (Galbraith, 1973, p. 219).

25. "It has always been a prime tenet of the neoclassical model that wants do not diminish in urgency and hence goods do not diminish in importance with increased output" (Galbraith, 1973, p. 158). Galbraith aligns that model with pretechnocratic capitalism.

26. I am not making the familiar point that economists proceed as though goods are always good and nothing else is. That is the complaint of Galbraith, Mishan, and others. The present point is different.

27. One distinguished economist at this conference made the extreme proposal that economics should be seen as the study of market transactions. If economics is also the study of economies, it would follow that there exists no noncapitalist economy and that there is therefore no need to say what sort of economy capitalism is.

28. Though to the extent that the Soviet Union attempts to overtake capitalism by taking over capitalist structures, or by letting capitalist

society take it over, the link I make between capitalism and output expansion is strengthened.

29. I have dealt only with the most manifest messages in favor of goods projected by capitalist society. To show how much else in its culture has the same end is more than I can do here.

REFERENCES

Ashton, T. S. (1948) *The Industrial Revolution, 1760-1830.* London: Oxford University Press.

Galbraith, J. K. (1967) *The New Industrial State.* Harmondsworth, England: Penguin.

Galbraith, J. K. (1973) *Economics and the Public Purpose.* London: Deutsch.

Lenin, V. I. (1967) "Karl Marx," *Selected Works* (Vol. 11). New York: International.

Marx, K. (1904) *A Contribution to The Critique of Political Economy.* Chicago: C. H. Kerr.

Marx, K. (1953) *Grundrisse der Kritik der Politischen Okonomie.* Berlin: Dietz.

Marx, K. (1961) *Capital* (Vol. 1). Moscow: Foreign Languages.

Marx, K. (1962) *Capital* (Vol. 3). In F. Engels (ed.) Moscow: Foreign Languages.

Marx, K. (1968) *Theories of Surplus Value* (Vol. 1). Moscow: Foreign Languages.

Marx, K. (1969) *Theories of Surplus Value* (Vol. 2). Moscow: Foreign Languages.

Marx, K. (1972) *Theories of Surplus Value* (Vol. 3). Moscow: Foreign Languages.

Marx, K. & Engels, F. (1958) *Selected Works* (Vol. 1). Moscow: Foreign Languages.

Mishan, E. J. (1967) *Costs of Economic Growth.* New York: Praeger.

Sklar, M. (May-June 1969) *Radical America* (Journal).

Weber, M. (1961) *General Economic History.* New York: Collier.

8

ETHICAL AND ECONOMIC ASPECTS OF GOVERNMENTAL INTERVENTION IN THE MEDICAL CARE MARKET

REUBEN A. KESSEL
University of Chicago

Medicine is a field characterized by many paradoxes. Americans study medicine abroad because of inadequate opportunities to study in the United States, while federal subsidies per physician produced in the United States exceed that of virtually every other academic skill. Income is redistributed from the poor to the well to do by both the state and federal governments in order to increase the output of physicians, while complaints of physician "shortages" are commonplace, and access to physician services, particularly in small towns and by the urban poor, is widely regarded as unsatisfactory. Access to medical care, it is commonly asserted, is a "right" and not a privilege, but slogans for parallel rights of access to food and clothing are rarely annunciated. Governmental intervention in the medical care market is stronger than it is in most markets, while governmental intervention in the food and clothing markets is, if anything, weaker than it is in most markets. The first part of this paper deals with these paradoxes and offers a rationale for their existence. The second provides evidence to support the explanation offered.

MEDICAL CARE VS. FOOD AND CLOTHING: RIGHTS TO ACCESS

We all recognize that our society has implicitly decided that standards of living in the United States will not fall below a certain preassigned level. This level has been rising secularly over time, and the current minimum level exceeds the average level in many countries of the world. This implicit decision about the standards of living is revealed by a fiscal commitment. We are prepared to reduce our disposable or after-tax income collectively in order to provide the means to maintain a desired minimum standard of living in our society.

The government and the taxing mechanisms may be viewed as instruments for achieving this desired minimum standard of living. However, it is clear that it is not the government that maintains this minimum; it is all of us collectively that do so, through self-imposed taxes and subsidies to the least affluent of our society. Indeed, many regard such redistribution as the most important activity that governments undertake.

For the execution of this redistributive function, it is important to recognize that it is not necessary that the government engage directly in the production or distribution of either food or clothing, or anything else that goes into what constitutes a "standard of living." This is especially true for medical care and education, two activities that the government is directly involved in producing and distributing.

The absence of slogans for food and clothing that are the counterpart of the slogan for medical care cannot be explained by the unwillingness of the community to provide medical care directly instead of providing funds to the poor and relying on the market. In our desire to provide for a minimum standard of living, we have relied on private, for-profit institutions much more extensively for food and clothing than for medical care.

Moreover, the existence of the slogan for medical care but not for food and clothing cannot be attributed to a niggardly attitude by society with respect to providing medical care for those who are the least fortunate in this society. If anything, we have higher standards for medical care than for food and clothing, which is evidenced by the fact that we have a category known as "medically indigent." Those belonging in this category receive assistance from society only for medical care. Our income cutoffs preclude assistance for food, clothing, shelter, and transportation, but not for medical care; the income levels at which Medicaid can be received are much higher than they are for other forms of assistance.

My purpose in pointing out the existence of the differing standards is not to argue for or against them. Whether or not we should have them is irrelevant for the theme to be developed here. I only wish to assert that this slogan exists, despite a higher minimum standard for medical care.

Perhaps it is unnecessary to point out that the slogan about rights to access to medical care has certain hidden implications. If someone has a right, then there exists a corresponding obligation in some unspecified, unknown person or persons. These rights are economic and, if they exist, then there must be corresponding obligations for most taxpayers. Hence, these rights are in effect granted to some individuals in our society by all of us collectively.

Those in the business of supplying medical care in their private capacities (that is, beyond their roles as taxpayers) have gone to special efforts to establish the rights to medical care. These efforts have no counterpart for those in the business of supplying food and clothing, which are supplied on the same terms for all income classes. In the provision of physician services, there exists in the literature, if not in reality, the view that physicians price discriminate so that they can provide care for poor or indigent patients.

This price discrimination theory implies that physicians operate their own taxing mechanism for redistributing from the well to do to the poor, wholly independent of the government's activities in this sphere. There is no counterpart to price discrimination in any other market. In addition to the redistributive services of physicians, hospitals solicit funds from the public either directly or through the government, typically via

Hill-Burton funds, in order to have facilities to provide care for those who, for one reason or another, are unable to provide care for themselves.[1]

Indeed, most major hospitals are organized as nonprofit institutions. In courts, they have occasionally won exceptions from the standards of performance expected of profit-seeking institutions utilizing the doctrine of charitable immunity. Again, there is no counterpart to the hospital in the food or clothing markets, which only deepens the paradox—providing medical care has received a great deal of special attention by taxpayers, both directly and indirectly, and by private charitable institutions as well as physicians acting as charitable institutions. Yet it is possible to observe much greater dissatisfaction with the way medical care is delivered than is true for food and clothing. The paradox continues to be unresolved because of the extent to which we have all collectively subsidized medical education. There currently exist federal subsidies to medical schools explicitly for the production of physicians.[2] Moreover, taxpayers in nearly every state of the United States, in their capacity as state citizens, have heavily subsidized medical education.

In general, most of us believe that subsidies, using the government as an intermediary, should go from the affluent to the poor. Needless to say, this principle has been violated many times and in many activities. However, in the subsidization of medical education, this principle is not violated; it is raped. The subsidization of medical education in the United States, to put matters baldly, constitutes a redistribution from lower- to higher-income classes. Admission to medical school in the United States is equivalent to admission to at least the upper 10 percent of the income distribution. The permanent income hypothesis, the view that the present worth of future earnings is the appropriate measure of the wealth position of an individual, implies that the income of medical students is transitorily low; this hypothesis also implies that it is their lifetime income that is relevant in evaluating the redistributive effects of subsidies to medical education. Yet, despite our willingness to subsidize the well to do if they are going to practice medicine, despite the development of charities engaged in the production and delivery of medical care, despite the private taxes physicians say they impose on their more affluent patients, there remains a great concern over access to medical care.

THE RIGHT OF ACCESS TO MEDICAL EDUCATION

In my view, the development of rights of access to medical care stem from the absence of another right—the right of those who wish to become physicians to have the opportunity to do so. In general, we subscribe to the view that we are willing to provide educational opportunities, at the expense of the tax-payer, to study almost anything from basket weaving to sports announcing. The single, dominant, and most powerful exception to this statement is medical education. We have not provided opportunities to study medicine in the United States that are on a par with those available for law, business, library science, civil work, engineering, etc.

The United States has a comparative advantage in higher education. According to the Institute on International Education field-by-field survey, there is only one field in which the number of foreigners studying in the United States does not exceed Americans studying abroad—undergraduate medical education. Moreover, for closely related fields such as biology, the comparative advantage of the United States is quite strong. It is an insufficiently appreciated fact that about 10 percent of all Americans studying medicine are studying abroad. It is very difficult to believe that they are studying abroad by choice. The schools are generally poorer abroad than they are in the United States, the language of instruction typically is not English, and the programs of study are usually six years and designed for students coming from high school. By contrast, the American studying abroad usually has completed an undergraduate education, and faces formidable and time-consuming problems of getting licensed in the United States after returning home. Americans studying medicine abroad are licensed at an average age of about five years older than their counterparts who study in the United States. Their earnings, once they become licensed, are lower than their domestically trained colleagues.

Why do we observe this paucity of educational opportunities in the United States for Americans to become physicians?[3] In my view, it is a result of the control over educational opportunities won by organized medicine shortly before World War I. The medical profession at that time viewed itself as being too large, with far too much free entry into both medicine and medical education, and set about rectifying what it regarded as a dreadful state of affairs.[4] With the aid of the Carnegie Foundation and the famous Flexner report on medical education (Flexner, 1910a), the medical profession induced state legislatures to turn over the right to rate medical schools to a wholly owned subdivision of the AMA and established graduation from one of these schools as a necessary condition for admission to licensure examinations.

Using these powers, the AMA undertook what probably constitutes the most radical surgery ever undertaken in American education. Schools were forced to merge or were put out of business, not because they were not viable in the market, but because of the desire to reduce numbers in the medical profession. By virtue of the power to bar graduates of unapproved medical schools from licensure exams, the marketability of the services of unapproved schools was destroyed. It is a little known and unappreciated fact that the frequency of blacks in medicine was rising sharply before the advent of the Flexner Report, and that five out of seven black medical schools were put out of business. Moreover, the absolute number of women in medicine in 1910 was not reached again for about three decades. Free entry was replaced by restricted entry; nondiscrimination in admissions was replaced by discrimination. For further documentation of this position, see Kessel (1970).

The restraints on opportunities to study medicine have been "sold" as a means of protecting the public against the ministrations of incompetent physicians. Studies showing that the public has in fact benefited from this protection seem to be difficult to find in medical literature. Indeed, it is reasonable to conclude that they are nonexistent. The absence of such studies is consistent with the way entry is restricted. If organized medicine were in fact concerned with standards, then admission to licensure examinations would not be restricted to graduates of approved schools, existing practitioners would be subject to relicensure examinations, and schools would not have been permitted in the past to exercise discrimination in terms of race, creed, or color in their admission policies. The fact that Linus Pauling, one of the great figures in biochemistry, could not be admitted to the medical licensure examinations in virtually every state in the United States (graduation from a medical school is a necessary condition for admission except for foreign medical graduates) illustrates the fallacy of the position that these regulations exist to protect the public against incompetent physicians.

GOVERNMENTAL INTERVENTION AND RIGHTS OF ACCESS TO MEDICAL CARE

To return to my thesis, the concern about rights of access to medical care today is related to a lack of concern in the past about rights of access to physician training. If we had been more concerned about these rights of access to physician training then, we would be far less concerned about access to medical care now.[5] As a result of this concern about access to medical care, we have politicians of both parties proposing and enacting legislation protecting and guaranteeing rights of access, a situation that is aptly described by Professor Ronald Coase's (1960) statement:

> The kind of situation which economists [and others] are prone to consider as requiring corrective Government action is, in fact, often the result of Governmental action. (p. 28)

The relevance of this quotation from Coase, even for medicine, is much broader than I have indicated. The balance of this chapter is devoted to an elaboration of this theme.

Prepaid Medical Plans

The Nixon Administration rechristened what formerly was known as "prepaid medical groups" or "closed-panel medicine"; the new name is "health maintenance organizations." In addition to rechristening this method of marketing medical care, the administration took some hesitant steps to promote the new organizations' formation as a means for controlling the costs of medical care. Not so long ago these plans were strongly and, unfortunately, effectively opposed by organized medicine by inducing state legislators to outlaw the existence of such plans. In effect, such legislation made the marketing of medical care by closed-panel groups an illegal activity and a victimless crime like prostitution. However, unlike prostitution, the illegal marketing of medical care was carefully enforced. If these laws had never been enacted, there is no doubt that there currently would exist many more such plans, and much of the current governmental effort to encourage their existence would be redundant (Kessel, 1958).

Eyeglass Prices

Professor Lee Benham's study of eyeglass prices in states that permit and those that do not permit price advertising shows that they are lower in states that permit advertising (Benham, 1972). This evidence suggests that statutory prohibition on advertising restrains competition and imposes higher prices of medical care upon consumers. Benham's evidence suggests that if statutory regulation of advertising pertaining to medical care were not enacted, prices would be lower. The prohibition of advertising has clearly deterred the formation of prepaid groups. To operate on a large scale, it is necessary to have a large throughput. To obtain this throughput, the ability to advertise is very important.

Blood

Our reliance upon voluntary agencies and charitable institutions in the delivery of medical care has not produced what most students of industrial organizations regard as highly competitive markets. However, it is often argued that they raise standards of care above what would be provided in their absence. Let me offer you what I regard as a strong piece of evidence against this point of view.

Suppose I asserted that there exists a product or, more properly, a complex of closely related products that are widely used by accident patients in trauma, although this is far from the only use of this complex of products. Moreover, the use of this product can and has on occasion transmitted diseases that have been fatal to patients. This complex of products is primarily collected and processed for medical use by volunteer agencies, although some drug companies also supply variants of this product.

Would you believe that the usual commercial standards that

apply to soup, clams, drugs, etc., are not applied to this product? Or, to put the same matter more directly, caveat emptor—let the buyer beware—is the prevailing doctrine under which this product is sold? The doctrine of caveat emptor has been applied to this product, while product liability has been generally growing in much of the commercial world. Moreover, it has been applied to a product about which consumers know little, a product whose quality could be more cheaply monitored by the seller than the buyer of medical services, and a product bought at times by a patient who is literally unconscious and obviously in no position to accept responsibility for the quality of the product being administered.

What is the product? It is blood and blood derivatives. The most costly disease transmitted by this product is transfusion hepatitis, or type-B hepatitis, although malaria, some forms of venereal disease, and type-A hepatitis have been transmitted.

How did this dreadful state of affairs come to pass, and why doesn't the government do something about it? The answer to these questions is that the government or, more properly, the state legislatures created the situation with the laws they have enacted. Many courts, including the courts in Illinois, Washington, Florida, Pennsylvania, and New Jersey have held for strict liability in tort when patients who have contracted transfusion hepatitis have sued hospitals and blood banks. In other words, the courts have held that the usual standards of product liability that exist in the commercial market are applicable to blood.

As a result of such legal decisions, the medical establishment, i.e., hospitals, blood banks, voluntary agencies such as the American Red Cross, and physicians have lobbied, unfortunately successfully, for laws eliminating product liability for blood. The laws enacted often use the legal circumlocution that a transfusion in a hospital is not a product but a service. These laws are a testimonial to the political power of these groups in state legislatures.

An unintended consequence of these laws is that the normal commercial standards applied to drug companies are inoperative for blood derivatives. To repeat, standards for particular drug company products are lower than they would be if the volunteer agencies were not in the blood business. Titmuss (1970) has complained that the low quality of blood transfused in the

United States vis-à-vis England, is attributable to too much commercialism. Assuming Titmuss' assertion of fact is correct, and serious questions can be raised on this point, it appears to be a result of too little commercialism.[6] It seems inconceivable that if blood suppliers had to stand behind their product, as they normally do in the commercial world, they would supply high-risk blood and blood-derivative products for transfusion. Moreover, the usual standards of supplier responsibility would exist for blood, if not for the political power of the medical establishment in state legislatures (Kessel, 1974).

Drugs

Still another aspect of state intervention in the provision of medical care is the introduction of new drugs. The federal government via the Food and Drug Administration (FDA) regulates the introduction of new drugs. Clearly, in an uncertain world, the FDA can commit either a type-one or type-two error. The evidence produced by Peltzman in his study of the introduction of new drugs clearly shows that the drugs are uneconomically delayed in their introduction. Alternatively, Peltzman's results show that fewer lives are saved by the discovery of adverse effects than are lost through the unavailability of drugs, given present governmental controls over the introduction of drugs.[7] An important implication of this intervention is the absence, or the degradation in quality, of treatments for particular ailments in the United States.

SUMMARY

In conclusion, let me repeat my theme: Our concern over the availability of medical care for the public is not the consequence of a natural phenomenon like a tornado or a hurricane. It is a consequence of governmental intervention in the supply of medical care. If this intervention had not occurred, we would currently be less concerned about rights or access to medical care. Moreover, we would not have foreclosed another right—the right to the opportunity to undertake the education to enter the medical profession. Finally, it is highly unlikely that we would have embarked upon a federal program to subsidize the rich in order to produce physicians.

Governmental intervention in a number of other markets associated with the provision of medical care has been shown not to benefit consumers. In blood, the normal protection afforded to buyers in commercial markets has been stripped away from consumers by legislative enactments. In some states, legislative prohibition on advertising has raised prices consumers must pay for eyeglasses. And in drugs, governmental regulation has either precluded or delayed the introduction of beneficial new drugs to consumers. However, the costs of delay have been estimated to exceed the benefits from foreclosing the introduction of harmful drugs.

The failure to have governmental representation of consumer interests in the medical care market is caused by an imperfection in the political marketplace. Despite the demonstration that the losses of consumers through state intervention are greater than the gains of producers, the producers nevertheless seem able to outbid consumers for the votes of legislators. This outcome can be attributed to the fact that consumers are many and diffuse and the transaction costs in pooling their resources to outbid producers, either with bribes or with campaign contributions, is enormous. Until this imperfection is eliminated, it is hard to believe that governmental intervention in the medical care market (and this proposition can be extended to other markets such as milk) will service consumer interests.

NOTES

1. This is something the hospitals have on occasion conveniently forgotten and there is some effort to bring this to their attention via litigation. See Silver (1974) for further information.

2. This began with the passage of the Health Professions Education Act of 1963 and shifted into high gear with the passage of the Comprehensive Health Manpower Training Act of 1973.

3. This has not always been the case. Flexner (1910b) complained of a physician "surplus" and too many opportunities for the study of medicine.

4. In Pritchett's (the head of the Carnegie Foundation at the time) introduction to Flexner (1910a, p. 19), he contends, if not complains, that there was overproduction of physicians for 25 years.

5. In recent years, concern with the paucity of educational opportunities in medicine has developed. Unfortunately, this concern has not gone to the root of the problem. See Kessel (1972).

6. Titmuss' standards of evidence leave something to be desired. There are differences in the average size of transfusions in the United States and United Kingdom, reporting standards, and problems about how well the studies cited by Titmuss represent the relevant populations. These problems he blithely ignored.

7. See Peltzman (1973, p. 113). Peltzman does not take up the question of who the beneficiaries of this policy are. It is not unreasonable to argue that it is the holders of existing and approved drug patents who gain.

REFERENCES

Benham, L. K. 1972. "The Effect of Advertising on the Price of Eyeglasses," *Journal of Law and Economics*, October.

Coase, R. 1960. "The Problem of Social Cost." *Journal of Law and Economics*. 3, 28.

Flexner, A. 1910a. *Medical Education in the United States and Canada.* Bull. No. 4. Carnegie Foundation.

Flexner, A. 1910b. "The Plethora of Doctors," *Atlantic Monthly*, 106, 20-25.

Kessel, R. A. 1970. "The AMA and the Supply of Physicians, Symposium on Health Care, Part I." *Law and Contemporary Problems*.

Kessel, R. A. 1972. "Higher Education and the Nation's Health: A Review of the Carnegie Commission Report on Medical Education," *Journal of Law and Economics*, April, p. 115.

Kessel, R. A. 1958. "Price Discrimination in Medicine," *Journal of Law and Economics*, 1, 20.

Kessel, R. A. 1974. "Transfused Blood, Serum Hepatitis, and the Coase Theorem," *Journal of Law and Economics*, October.

Peltzman, S. 1973. "The Benefits and Costs of New Drug Regulation," in R. L. Landau, ed., *Regulating New Drugs*. Chicago: University of Chicago, Center for Policy Study.

Silver, L. H. 1974. "The Legal Accountability of Nonprofit Hospitals," in C. C. Havighurst, ed., *Regulating Health Facilities Construction*. Washington, D.C.: American Enterprise Institute for Public Policy Research.

Titmuss, R. M. 1970. *The Gift Relationship: From Human Blood to Social Policy*. London: Allen and Unwin.

9

FREEDOMS AND UTILITIES IN THE DISTRIBUTION OF HEALTH CARE

PETER SINGER
Monash University, Victoria, Australia

Should the goods and services required to preserve and restore our health be bought and sold in the marketplace, like television sets and haircuts, or should they be provided in some other way? To completely answer this question, we would have to take into account a wide variety of considerations. We would need to inquire into the economics of alternative 'schemes for providing health care since we could not reach a proper decision unless we knew whether one scheme cost significantly less than the others. We would also need information of a sociological nature, i.e., who would receive care under the different schemes, and what kind of care? Even after we had all the economic and

As the body of this chapter shows, I am deeply indebted to the late Richard Titmuss, whose writings have provided me with most of the information and ideas that follow.

sociological information that we could reasonably expect to acquire, however, some very fundamental questions would remain—those of ethics. What are our ends or values? What are we trying to achieve in this area? What are the values or principles that should guide our conception of a good society, and how does this conception affect our choice of method?

It is these ethical questions that I am going to discuss. Since they cannot be considered in isolation from economic and sociological issues, I shall be referring to these areas, but my focus will be ethical.

Ethical questions are notoriously difficult to discuss fruitfully. There are no universally accepted ultimate principles or standards, and so many people seem to think that all they can do is state their own view as plausibly as they can and hope others will accept it. I do not believe that we are always forced to take quite so subjective an approach. In some areas of ethics, at least, argument is possible, and there are the usual standards of good and bad argument. Thus, we do not have to be content with appeals to emotion or intuition. In this chapter, I shall concentrate on these areas of ethics, where argument is possible and discussion can be fruitful. As far as health care is concerned, the main issues of this sort are, I believe, those involving freedom and utility. Before I move on to discuss these questions, however, I should first mention some of the ethical considerations I am leaving aside—considerations that many people think are important to the topic. I do not deny their importance, though I do not affirm it either. I am merely concerned to say that they are matters on which people disagree, and about which reasoned argument is scarce and fruitful discussion difficult to achieve.

HEALTH CARE AS A RIGHT

It is very common nowadays for those dissatisfied with the market approach to the distribution of health care to claim that "health care is a right." Thus, Senator Abraham Ribicoff, a leading campaigner for health care reform in the United States and chairman of a Senate subcommittee that has investigated aspects of medical care, argues that the most basic need is for "a new way of thinking about medical care, a philosophy that states our belief that to receive medical care is the individual's right, but to provide it is the nation's privilege" (Ribicoff, 1972, p. 10).

It would not be difficult to find other expressions of this idea. The phrase has a forceful ring to it and makes a fine slogan. If we interpret the slogan as saying that everyone should have a legal right to free health care, we have no problem in understanding the claim, although of course argument is needed to back it up; but if we try to take it literally, as though this idea in itself were all the justification needed for making health care a legal right, we will find it difficult to know what to make of this claim.

How are we to establish that health care really is a right? Argument soon comes to a halt. It is impossible to get people to agree on any list of natural or human rights once we get beyond the right to life, and even that is rarely held to be absolute. Other rights, such as the right to vote, depend on a particular political context. So-called welfare rights, of which the right to health care would be one, are more puzzling still, since they require not merely that others leave the individual alone but also that others take some positive action to provide the individual with something. So, while we can, in almost any circumstances, claim that to kill someone without his consent is to violate his right to life, we can speak meaningfully of a violation of a right to health care only if a society has reached the level of sophistication at which it has the means and knowledge to provide health care for everyone. That it is possible to talk of a "right to health care" depends on available resources; this suggests, however, that it is a right that must be balanced against other possible uses of those resources. And this suggests that whether or not we finally decide to recognize a right to health care will depend on a complex assessment of the benefits of providing free health care, as compared with the benefits of alternative systems of health care distribution. All this suggests that it is more fruitful to discuss these benefits, and their concomitant drawbacks, than to discuss the abstract philosophical issues of the nature of human rights, and whether health care is one of them.

DISTRIBUTIVE JUSTICE

A second claim that has seemed to settle the problem of whether health care should be taken out of the marketplace is that it is obviously unjust to provide health care on any grounds other than those of need. Justice, it is commonly and I think correctly said, demands that we treat like cases alike, except when there is a relevant difference between them. In the case of the distribution of health care, is it not self-evident that the only relevant consideration is how great a person's need for care is? Money—how wealthy a person is—obviously has nothing at all to do with whether he should receive medical care.

This argument appears plausible, but if it is intended to show that health care is a special case, peculiarly unsuited to the market mode of distribution, the argument proves far too much. It can be applied with equal plausibility to other areas. Is it not also obvious that the only relevant considerations governing the distribution of automobiles are those such as how difficult it would be for a person to get around without one, how well his neighborhood is served by public transportation, how much he needs to travel, and so on? How much money a person has is, by these standards, quite irrelevant. In other words, once we embark on this path of distributing goods and services on the basis of what is "obviously" fitting or relevant, there is no stopping place, short of Marx's vision of a society governed by the principle "From each according to his ability, to each according to his need" (Marx, 1875/1938). We may, of course, follow the argument where it leads, and say that it is applicable all the way: all goods and services should be distributed on the basis of need, rather than ability to pay. Personally, I think this really is an ideal form of distribution, if it can be made to work, but because it is a general principle, it cannot be invoked by those who claim that health care is *specially* unsuited to the marketplace. If ability to pay is sometimes relevant to how goods or services should be distributed, why is it irrelevant in this particular case? Within the normal assumptions of a market economy, ability to pay for a service is a relevant consideration that distinguishes between cases that are otherwise alike. While we may object to these market assumptions, I do not think that a discussion of considerations of abstract justice is likely to help us understand why people have thought it more important to take the distribution of health care, rather than the distribution of, say, automobiles, out of the market.

INTRINSIC EVIL

Finally, in this list of unfruitful approaches is the idea that it is somehow an intrinsic evil to make a commodity out of something essential for life. The feeling seems to be particularly strong when people discuss such questions as whether human blood should be sold or whether it is right for medical schools to pay people who will sign over their bodies, when they die, for teaching or research purposes. As the remainder of this chapter will make clear, I am opposed to making a commodity out of human blood. I am opposed, however, not because I think human blood is intrinsically not a commodity and there is evil in making it one, but because I believe the consequences of permitting the sale of human blood are worse than those of not doing so. I do not know how it is possible to make a rational case for the position that a particular thing is "intrinsically not a commodity." Once again, it seems to me this position can be defended only if it is made general. To say that intrinsically *nothing* is a commodity seems sound; but how one could argue that food is intrinsically a commodity while blood is not, I have no idea. On the other hand, if we ask why people feel that blood and bodies are not commodities—a psychological question, not a moral one—the answer may have something to do with the consequences of treating them as commodities and, in particular, the subtle effects this may have on the nature of the community that so treats them. About this I shall have a good deal more to say shortly.

I now move on to the first of the issues that I think can be discussed fruitfully.

FREEDOM

Defenders of the marketplace as a method of distributing goods and services, including health care, are most often those who see themselves as defenders of freedom. One example is F. A. Hayek (1960); Milton Friedman (1962) is another. The case of health care allows us to examine the assumption that leaving distribution to the market does increase freedom.

To make a clear contrast between market and nonmarket systems of distribution in the field of health care, it would be useful to compare the two systems in their pure forms. If we are considering the field of health care as a whole, however, this is not easy to do, since we do not have, in any major industrialized nation, a pure example of market distribution. In debates on whether to introduce some form of national health insurance or national health service in the United States, the assumption is often made that the issue is whether to continue to allow the laws of the market to operate in this area. However, this assumption overlooks the extent to which health care is already protected from the free and open competition that is an essential element of the marketplace.

Kenneth Arrow (1963), in his widely discussed article "Uncertainty and the Welfare Economics of Medical Care," has noted several aspects in which the medical care market in this country differs from the usual commodity markets (see also Titmuss, 1968, pp. 145–147). First, the demand for medical care is, preventive services apart, irregular and unpredictable, unlike practically every other item of significance in the average household budget. The need for the service may come suddenly, and one may not be in a position to shop around. Nor can the cost of the care that will be needed often be predicted in advance. Next, the ethics of the medical profession make medical care unlike other businesses. Doctors do not advertise, and there is no open price competition among them. A doctor who advises further treatment is supposed to be entirely unaffected by considerations of self-interest. Further, the existence of a medical profession severely limits the supply of medical care, for practitioners must be licensed. (This in itself is not unusual, but in the field of medicine, education plays an especially important role in limiting the number of doctors available; limited entry to medical school controls the number there will be in future years, but these decisions, despite their great influence on the state of the market, are made by nonprofit institutions.) Thus, the supply of medical care is not directly affected by the profitability of providing it, as would be the case in a normal market. A further consequence of this situation is a restriction of the range of quality of care available to the consumer. In a competitive market, different qualities of service would be offered at different prices, and the consumer could choose among them. Other differences between medical care and most commodities are that the consumer cannot learn reliably from experience, whether his own or that of friends, whether the care offered by a particular doctor or hospital was satisfactory. The factor of care received cannot be isolated from unknowables such as the patient's own recuperative powers. Finally, medical care cannot be returned to the seller for a money-back refund; it cannot even lightly be taken back for repairs if it goes wrong; nor can one cut one's losses and throw it away.

It is worth noting that many of these features that differentiate medical care from other commodities are the work of professional bodies such as, in this country, the American Medical Association. Although the AMA strongly opposes any move away from the status quo toward a national health service, the organization is equally firm in its opposition to move toward more open competition and effective consumer choice. Officials of the AMA have sometimes tried to present the doctor as "essentially a small businessman" who sells his services and so "is as much in business as anyone else who sells a commodity" (Dr. F. G. Dickenson, Head of the AMA Bureau of Medical Economic Research, quoted in Titmuss, 1968, p. 249). When Ralph Nader's consumer research organization took this idea seriously, however, and tried to compile a consumer's directory of doctors in Prince George's County, Maryland, listing doctors' fees, qualifications, office hours, and so on, the county medical society sent a letter to its members advising them not to cooperate and warning of possible sanctions against those who did. (Incidentally, the incomplete survey that resulted, as reported in *Village Voice*, 1974, was enough to reveal some remarkable variations in fees that consumers would have had difficulty discovering for themselves. For example, for sending a throat culture to a laboratory for a standard test, fees ranged from $3 to $16.50.)

There can be no freedom without adequate information on

which to base a choice. Clearly, consumers would have more freedom if they were better informed about items like fees. We could also expect that competition of this kind would lead to some reduction in fees. But before we conclude that this move is desirable from the point of view of freedom, we need to take into account the effect it could have on medical practice.

In an open market, the individual doctor would be less secure economically than at present. Economic considerations would therefore become more prominent in the doctor's relationship with the patient. The patient would be aware of this, and might be more likely than at present to suspect considerations of self-interest when the doctor advised frequent visits or further treatment. So, market considerations could undermine the relationship between doctor and patient. The AMA places a great deal of emphasis on this relationship, and I believe it is right to do so. Medical practice would be changed for the worse if the patient could not trust the doctor, confident that the doctor's only motivation was concern for the patient's well-being.

Let us look at an example of what may happen when the ethical relationship between doctor and patient breaks down. The increasingly impersonal and businesslike nature of medical practice in the United States appears to be reflected in the huge rise in the number of medical malpractice lawsuits. The more people travel around, change doctors, or see specialists with whom they establish no personal contact, the more likely they are to sue if anything goes wrong (Ribicoff, 1972, p. 116; see also *Medical Malpractice*, 1969, and *Report of the Secretary's Commission*, 1973). Doctors, of course, insure themselves against malpractice suits. One result of the rising number of cases brought is that premiums for malpractice insurance have now gone sky high. Insurance premiums for some doctors have risen by 500% since the malpractice crisis in the United States gathered steam in 1974. In California obstetricians and gynaecologists are now paying premiums of around $26,000 per annum compared with $6,000 in 1975. For surgeons and neurologists premiums can go as high as $60,000, (*National Times*). This annual expenditure must be recovered in increased fees from patients. Even at these rates, insurance companies are dropping out of the business because it is unprofitable. In January 1974, the company that had underwritten almost all malpractice insurance for New York State doctors decided to terminate its group policy. Nationally, more than 16,000 suits were filed in 1972, with settlements ranging up to $1 million (*New York Times*, 1974).

By comparison, in Britain, medical practitioners are covered against lawsuits for negligence by a subscription to the Medical Defence Union. In 1973, the most recent year for which I have figures, the subscription was the equivalent of $40 a year, and the society handled 236 cases of alleged negligence. While there are obviously other important differences between the two countries that could explain this startling variation, it is possible that when doctors are taken out of the marketplace, patients are less likely to treat them like other suppliers of commodities who fail to deliver. If this is the case, then to move toward more open competition among doctors would only aggravate the situation in the United States. More open competition would probably lead people to change doctors more frequently, and this in itself would damage the relationship between doctor and patient.

In the long run, ordinary consumers suffer the most from the high incidence of malpractice suits. It is they who must bear the brunt of the costs. Malpractice suits do not adequately protect them against incompetent doctors, since doctors almost invariably continue to practice after malpractice decisions go against them. Moreover, to keep down their premiums, doctors now tend to practice "legally defensive medicine," ordering batteries of unnecessary X rays and other tests, consulting with specialists and other doctors, all in order to cover themselves against a possible lawsuit. This causes inconvenience for the patient and, once again, higher medical fees. The only real beneficiaries of malpractice suits are the lawyers, who may take up to 50 percent of any award they win. Otherwise, individual patients who win cases may gain, but patients as a whole lose (Ribicoff, 1972, chap. 5; see also Titmuss, 1970, pp. 167–170).

The point of this discussion of malpractice litigation is that an attempt to increase the patient's freedom of choice in one area may, without his knowing it, compel him to accept a type of medical care that he would never voluntarily have chosen. If medical care were to become a commodity like any other, the consumer would be able to make a more informed choice among doctors on the basis of fees charged, but he might also be told to have tests that he would not have had were the doctor not so concerned about self-protection. In the end, the patient will have to pay a greatly inflated medical bill. It is reasonable to suppose that these practices will contribute to the further deterioration of the relationship between doctor and patient. The doctor can hardly reveal to the patient the true reason he is being sent to a specialist or to have an X ray. The patient may fear that more is wrong than the doctor has said. Alternatively, he may suspect that the doctor is trying to make money from it all. The ethics of any relationship are easier when nothing is hidden.

If consequences anything like those just sketched were to flow from a decision to increase competition in medical care—and I freely admit that no link has been proven—we would have to think again before we decided that more competition would mean more freedom for the patient. If no patient would voluntarily choose the more competitive system with its attendent disadvantages, an increase of competition appears to be coercive rather than liberating.

BLOOD AND FREEDOM

There has been a lot of speculation in what I have been saying up to now. We do not have, in any countries that are even roughly comparable, systems of medical care that represent the extremes of market and nonmarket distribution. There is, however, one aspect of medical care that does allow us to compare systems that come close to being pure forms of market and nonmarket systems. I am referring to systems of obtaining human blood for medical purposes. In Britain, blood is obtained by means far removed from the market. It is neither bought nor sold, but rather it is given, voluntarily and without reward beyond a cup of tea and a biscuit, by ordinary citizens. It is available to anyone who needs it, without charge, and without obligation. Donors gain no preference over nondonors if they need blood. Since enough is available for all, donors need no preference. Nor do donors have any hope of return favors from recipients, not even a grateful smile. Although the gift is in one way a very intimate one—the blood that now flows in the donor's veins will soon flow in the recipient's—the donor will never know whom he has helped. It is a gift from one stranger to another. The system is as close to a perfect example of institutionalized generosity and concern for one's fellows as can be imagined.

In the United States, only about 7 percent of the blood obtained for medical purposes comes from similarly voluntary donations. Around 40 percent is given to avoid having to pay for blood received, or to build up credit so that blood will be available without charge if needed. Approximately half of the blood and plasma obtained is bought and sold on a strictly commercial basis, like any other commodity. So completely commercial, in fact, is the operation of the commercial blood banks that when hospitals in Kansas City chose to get blood exclusively from a nonprofit community blood bank rather than from either of two commercial banks operating in the city, the commercial banks complained to the Federal Trade Commission. In due course, the commission ruled that the community bank and the hospitals had illegally conspired to restrain commerce in whole human blood, and ordered them to stop doing so—this, despite testimony that the commercially obtained blood carried a greater risk of infecting recipients with hepatitis than did the blood from the nonprofit bank.

These contrasting systems of blood collection provide us with the opportunity to ask whether the market leads to greater freedom in this area. I shall also, later, use the comparison to examine other differences between the systems, in terms of the values they further. The important thing about this comparison is that, for once, we not only can ask the questions, but also must try to answer them on the basis of some solid evidence. Thanks to Titmuss's (1970) absorbing study of the subject, we now have facts and figures, as well as Titmuss's own remarkable insights, to guide us. (I have discussed some of the following issues in Singer, 1973.)

Freedom takes a variety of forms. We cannot quantify it, and so there is no immediately obvious answer to the question, "Which system provides the greater freedom?" All I can do is indicate different directions in which freedom is enhanced or diminished.

If we ask, "Under which system does the individual have the freedom to choose whether to give or sell his blood?" the answer must be that this freedom is possible only where there is a commercial blood supply system as well as a voluntary one. This aspect of the situation is the basis of the orthodox economists' claim, as stated by Arrow (1972), that

> since the creation of a market increases the individual's area of choice, it therefore leads to higher benefits. Thus, if to a voluntary blood donor system we add the possibility of selling blood, we have only expanded the individual's range of alternatives. If he derives satisfaction from giving, it is argued that he can still give, and nothing has been done to impair that right. (pp. 349–350)

According to this orthodox economic view of freedom, once we see that the market creates this additional "freedom to sell," we need to look no farther, concerning the question of freedom. Why, these economists would argue, should we prevent those who choose to do so from getting the market price for their blood, rather than giving it away? Is it not a blatant infringement of the freedom of individuals to prevent them from doing something that harms no one? Moreover, the result of allowing the market to operate freely will, these economists believe, be beneficial in other respects, such as cost and quality of supply.

In reply to this claim, Titmuss has argued that while a commercial system allows freedom to sell, it denies citizens their freedom to give. The notion of social rights, Titmuss (1970, p. 242) said, should embrace "the right to give" in both material and nonmaterial ways.

Here, it seems to me that Titmuss has not expressed himself with sufficient clarity. Arrow denies the existence of any incompatibility between the right to give and the right to sell, and indeed it is not strictly accurate to say that the existence of a commercial system alongside a voluntary one denies anyone the right to give voluntarily. If we choose to give, we may do so, even when others are selling. The simple right to give remains intact.

What is it, then, that Titmuss had in mind when he claimed that the existence of a commercial system denies the right to give? The point is worth exploring, because it reveals the limits of the orthodox economists' notion of freedom.

In the language of orthodox economists, we enlarge a person's freedom if we increase the choices open to him. It does not matter *why* someone chooses as he does. As long as he is able to choose, the choice is regarded as a reflection of his preferences. In fact, the economist defines a person's preferences, or "revealed preferences," in terms of what he chooses. This is supposed to make economics a value-free science. Why the individual chooses as he does is something the economist is not concerned with. The goal is to give everyone what he prefers— never mind why he prefers what he does, or whether he will be happier once he has it.

This notion of freedom is superficial in the most literal sense of the term; it refuses to probe beneath the surface. In the particular case we are considering, this notion of freedom is satisfied in the American situation because a person can give blood voluntarily *if* he chooses to do so. It is, in this notion of freedom, irrelevant to consider that, as Titmuss showed, the existence of a commercial system may discourage voluntary donors. It appears to discourage them, but not because those who would otherwise have donated their blood voluntarily choose to sell it instead if this alternative is available. In fact, donors and sellers are, in the main, different sections of the population. Rather, voluntary donors are discouraged because the blood's availability as a commodity, to be bought and sold, affects the nature of the gift that is made when blood is donated. If blood is a commodity with a price, to give blood seems merely to save someone money; it has a cash value of a certain number of dollars. As such, the importance of the gift will vary with the wealth of the recipient. If blood cannot be bought, however, then its value as a gift depends on the recipient's need. Often, it will be worth life itself. Under these circumstances, giving blood becomes very special, an act of providing for strangers, without hope of reward, something they cannot buy and without which they may die. The gift relates strangers in the community in a manner that is not possible when blood is a commodity.

All this may seem removed from the real world of ordinary people and hard facts. It is not. It is something ordinary people can be as much aware of as can the most unworldly philosopher. It is an idea spontaneously expressed by British blood donors themselves, in response to a questionnaire in which Titmuss asked them why they had first decided to become blood donors.

As one woman, a machine operator, wrote in reply:

> You cant get blood from the supermarkets and chaine stores. People them selves must come forward, sick people cant get out of bed to ask you for a pint to save thier life so I came forword in hope to help somebody who needs blood [sic].

A company secretary answered with better spelling, but less warmth:

> I feel that with blood it would have to be used for the purposes it was given, no deductions for administrative purposes like so many Charity Organizations. Blood is something which could not come out of the rates.

Other donors expressed a wish to help the National Health Service. In some cases, they said they had been helped either by the health service generally or by blood transfusions specifically, and they now wanted to do something in return. With others, the motivation was that they might themselves sometime need the assistance of a stranger, and if they were then to have a moral right to receive it, they felt that they should themselves give when they had the opportunity (Titmuss, 1970, pp. 226-236).

The implication of some of these answers is clear: even if these people had had the formal right to give to a voluntary program that existed alongside commercial blood banks, their gift would have lost much of its significance, and they might well not have given at all. The fact that blood is a commodity, that it can still be bought if no one gives it, makes altruism unnecessary, and so loosens the bonds that can otherwise exist between strangers in the community.

The accuracy of this interpretation of the effect of a commercial blood system on a voluntary one is borne out by statistics on voluntary donations in England and Wales, as compared with countries such as the United States and Japan, where commercial systems now exist. In all these countries, there has been a sharp rise in the need for blood in recent years. In England and Wales, donations have increased sufficiently to cover this increased demand, and the National Blood Transfusion Board "has never consciously been aware of a shortage, or an impending shortage, of potential donors" (Titmuss, 1970, p. 120). In the United States, on the other hand, not only have voluntary donations failed to keep pace with the increased demand, but they have actually fallen in absolute terms. In New York, for instance, the only city to have published sufficient figures to indicate a trend, voluntary community donations fell from 20 percent of total supplies in 1956 to 1 percent in 1966. Commercial supplies have not risen enough to compensate for this fall, and serious shortages have resulted, frequently forcing postponement of surgery (Titmuss, 1970, pp. 39–40, 59, 96).

In Japan, the decline in voluntary donors has been still more abrupt. Apparently, donors were not paid until 1951, when the need to supply blood to American forces in Korea led to the introduction of payment. Now 98 percent of all blood is paid for, and the shortage of blood is said to be still more critical than in the United States (Titmuss, 1970, p. 156).

So, it appears that where payment for blood does not exist, the number of donors has kept pace with the sharp rise in demand, but where the opportunity to give is forced to coexist with the opportunity to sell, the number of volunteers declines and the resulting shortage can be made good only with difficulty, if at all, by increasing the amount of blood bought. A reasonable conclusion to draw from these facts is that to make blood a commodity discourages voluntary donors, while a purely voluntary system fosters altruism in a way that a mixed commercial and voluntary system does not.

The meaning of all this, as far as freedom is concerned, is complex. I have already conceded that the creation of a commercial system alongside a voluntary one allows people to sell their blood, while leaving them formally free to give it voluntarily, if they so desire. But Titmuss's idea that the creation of a commercial system threatens the right to give is not so much mistaken as inadequately developed. The right that Titmuss saw threatened is not the simple right to give, but the right to give "in nonmaterial as well as material ways." This means not merely the right to give money or some commodity that can be bought or sold for a certain amount of money, but the right to give something that cannot be bought, that has no cash value, and must be given freely if it is to be obtained at all. This right, if it is a right (it would be better to say "this freedom"), really is incompatible with the freedom to sell, and we cannot avoid denying one of these freedoms when we grant the other.[1]

Even if we discount the value of this "freedom to give in nonmaterial terms," I think the facts I have presented bear out my claim that the orthodox economists' notion of freedom is superficial. What is more important, whether Americans have the formal freedom to give their blood, if they so desire, or whether the conditions under which blood may be given are such as to tap the resources of altruism and community feeling that Americans may be presumed to have to the same degree as Britons? The fact that many people who would otherwise give blood will not do so if it can be bought should not be ignored or brushed aside. To say that this decision is the individual's free choice, and that freedom is maximized as long as a person can give if he chooses to do so, is to take a naïve view of the nature of choice. We know that social circumstances affect individual choices. Therefore, we must either deepen our notion of freedom, to recognize that certain kinds of social conditions restrict freedom, or else acknowledge that freedom is an idea with form but no substance. If we take the latter view, it would seem that freedom, considered apart from the circumstances in which it is exercised, is less important than it is usually thought to be. In my opinion it is the former course that is the sounder one. In deepening our notion of freedom, we recognize that the individual does not decide in a vacuum, and that the social policies we pursue affect the decisions individuals make. We cannot say that these policies will determine the decision of any given individual, but we know that statistically they will alter a number of decisions. Knowing this, we cannot pretend we do not know it and say that by not interfering with the market we are leaving the decision up to the individual. The decision not to interfere affects individual choices, just as the decision to interfere does.

BLOOD AND UTILITY

Titmuss's study of blood supply systems helps us to explore other issues, apart from freedom, that are important to the whole area of health care. In particular, it enables us to assess the utility of market and nonmarket systems and to ask which leads to the greater good in the long run.

Long ago, Marx (1844/1967) suggested that money, by converting human requirements into commodities, degrades and dehumanizes us:

> If money is the bond binding me to human life, binding society to me, binding me and nature and man, is not money the bond of all bonds? Can it not dissolve and bind all ties? Is it not, therefore, the universal agent of separation? . . . Money then appears as this over-turning power both against the individual and against the bonds of society, etc., which claim to be essences in themselves. It transforms fidelity into infidelity, love into hate, hate into love, virtue into vice. . . . Assume man to be man and his relationship to the world to be a human one: then you can exchange love only for love, trust for trust, etc. (pp. 167–169)

The area of blood supply offers remarkably concrete illustrations of Marx's insight. We have already seen that the market may hamper the expression of a desire to help strangers. It can also be shown, very simply, that the market in this area does indeed turn truth into falsity, virtue into vice, and a life-saving gift into a deadly poison.

Not all blood is of the same quality. Some diseases can be passed from donor to recipient in a transfusion. It is possible to test for some diseases in a laboratory, but not for all. Of those impossible to check for, by far the most important is serum hepatitis. The only way to eliminate or substantially reduce the risk of transmitting it to blood recipients is to ask donors or sellers about their medical history and social habits. When asked these questions, the voluntary donor has no reason to lie, for he does not want his gift to harm anyone. His interests and those of the recipient are in harmony. The would-be seller, however, does have an incentive to lie. If he tells the truth he may be unable to sell his commodity. His private interests conflict with those of the recipient of his blood. The resulting lack of truthfulness, combined with the higher incidence of hepatitis in blood sellers than in the population as a whole, produces an occurrence of hepatitis following transfusion of commercially obtained blood that is many times higher than that following transfusion of donated blood. One carefully controlled study of patients undergoing cardiac surgery, in which an average of 18 or 19 pints of blood are used, showed the incidence of hepatitis in a group receiving commercial blood to be 55 percent, while a similar group receiving voluntarily donated blood had no cases at all. Although such exceptionally high rates occur only when a lot of blood is used, only one pint of which needs to be infected, other studies suggest a general rate of infection at least four times as high in the United States as in Britain, while in Japan the situation is much worse still (Titmuss, 1970, chap. 7). There seems to be no means by which the market mechanism can equal the performance of the voluntary system in this respect.

There are other areas in which the voluntary system works better than its rival. We have already seen that the voluntary system has been able to procure enough blood to meet rising needs, while commercial systems have not. (The United States, incidentally, is now starting to import some blood from Latin America, whose inhabitants need money more than do U.S. citizens, but who have less protein to replace what they give.) The voluntary system also produces blood more cheaply than do commercial systems. Titmuss estimated that the overall cost of a pint of blood is between 5 and 15 times higher when the blood is obtained commercially in the United States than when it is obtained through voluntary donations in Britain. (In the United States this cost is borne by the consumer; in Britain the overheads of the National Transfusion Service are paid out of general taxation.)

In addition to these straightforward advantages, there is also a more subtle one. The nature of a community depends on the nature of the people who make it up, and this in turn depends to some extent on its institutions and the attitudes these institutions foster. Institutions that put a money value on everything, that restrict ways in which strangers can help each other, and that set the interest of one person against those of another, are consonant with a materialistic community in which each looks out only for his own interests. Such institutions are both the product of such a society and a factor in its continuance. Institutions that facilitate the expression of a desire to help others and distribute goods according to need are a means of preserving and fostering attitudes of concern for one's fellows. Controlled experiments suggest that people are more likely to behave altruistically when they observe altruism in others;[2] on a personal level I have found that nothing brings out my better impulses as well as being with others who habitually act out of generosity and consideration for others. A society with institutions that foster altruism may therefore expect to reap further benefits. There may be no direct link between the amount of blood donated voluntarily in London and New York and the crime rates in these cities; but both sets of figures point in the same direction, and they say similar things about human relations in the two cities.

Let us now turn our attention from this particular aspect of health care back to health care in general. Prior to embarking on the discussion of blood supply systems, I drew attention to some of the consequences that might follow from making health care more competitive than it is at present in the United States. I think I have raised sufficient doubts about the desirability of so doing. Should we then take medical care out of the marketplace altogether? Is the British National Health Service a model to follow as the British National Transfusion Service is? Somewhat different issues are raised by this question; and in the space that remains, I shall be able to discuss only some of them, and rather briefly.

A NATIONAL HEALTH SERVICE?

A national health service must be financed by taxation. It does, therefore, limit the taxpayer's freedom to decide how much to spend on health, and how much on other items. Of course, other welfare measures, such as social security do the same, in their own area. There is, however, a prima facie case against such a restriction. What can be said in defense of the restriction in this case?

First, it may be that the community, acting together, can achieve health care goods that the individual cannot achieve, no matter how much he decides to spend. We have already seen examples of this in respect to obtaining cheap, uncontaminated blood and obtaining medical services that have not been distorted by the threat of malpractice suits. There are many other ways in which the special nature of medical care may make it unsuited to market control. For instance, the market's answer to the uncertainty of an individual's need for extensive medical care is private insurance. Private insurance, however, tends to be extremely expensive for ordinary visits to a doctor, because doctors, in the privacy of their offices, are not subject to supervision from peers or anyone else, and so might prescribe unnecessary treatments in order to increase their remuneration from the insurance company. One consequence of this is that most people are insured for hospital visits, but not for office visits; and a consequence of this is that some medical care now takes place in hospitals that could be done more economically in the patient's home or the doctor's office. The ultimate consequence is that the consumer pays more for medical insurance.

This difficulty is not one that can be eliminated simply by a system of national health insurance like those envisaged in recent congressional bills. These proposals would retain the principle of paying the doctor for each treatment, and this would leave the system wide open to abuse if it covered surgery visits, unless there were a huge and expensive system of inspectors. On the other hand, if the scheme does not cover surgery visits, it will accelerate the trend to increased hospitalization.

This problem can be avoided under a national health service by paying the doctors on some basis other than the cost of the treatment they prescribe. In Britain, for example, doctors are paid according to the number of patients on their roll, with a lower payment per patient after a certain figure is reached, to discourage excessively large rolls, and an absolute ceiling at a higher point, to prohibit unworkably large practices. Admittedly, there are drawbacks to this method too, for doctors get paid even if they do very little for their patients. A complaints procedure and the possibility of patients' transferring to other doctors may curb this tendency. A more important restraint is the bond of an ethical relationship between doctor and patient that has not been eroded by the commercialization of medical practice.

Another frequently cited drawback of proposals for either a national health service or national insurance is that patients have no disincentive to prevent them from visiting doctors as often as they like, since they do not pay for it. In fact, British statistics do not bear out this fear; although the figures are not comprehensive enough to give a decisive answer, they do not appear to show any rise in demand per patient since the inauguration of the National Health Service (Titmuss, 1963, p. 174).[3] Perhaps the explanation for this is that the overuse one might expect from a few people is balanced by the practice of preventive medicine. Prevention is, as the saying goes, better than cure; and patients who go for a regular checkup, or when they first notice something wrong, may in the end be much less expensive to treat than those who put off a visit to the doctor until they are seriously ill. One thing certain is that Britain spends a smaller percentage of its gross national product on health care than the United States does, despite the fact that health care is free to all in Britain. Quite apart from expense, though, is the question of how many cases of overuse are needed to offset one patient who dies because he postponed seeking treatment in order to save money.

Another possible justification for a national health service is that it is an effective means of redistributing income, since it may be paid for by a progressively graduated income tax and distributed to all irrespective of income. The poorest, especially, are helped, since they will pay little or no tax and receive essential services they could not otherwise afford. It is hardly necessary to describe the distress a person may feel who requires medical care but is unable to afford it. The security and peace of mind that arises from knowing that one will never be in this situation is one of the greatest benefits a society can bestow on its poorer citizens. Indeed, the heights that medical expenses have reached in this country recently mean that it is not only the poor, but also those in the middle income bracket, who require this security. Senator Ribicoff (1972) cites the case of a family who received a bill of $4,600 for the four and one-half days their father had been in hospital before he died. Medical bills are now a major factor in bankruptcies; in Tulsa, Oklahoma, a survey showed that they account for 60 percent of all bankruptcies (Ribicoff, 1972, pp. 11-12).

Conservative economists are not necessarily opposed to some measure of redistribution, especially if it is designed to improve the condition of the very poor. Friedman (1962) goes so far as to advocate a negative income tax; this would mean redistribution in cash rather than services. Friedman prefers cash because he thinks it makes for more freedom, allowing the individual to spend his money as he likes. He may choose to spend it on health insurance, or he may choose whatever else he wants.

I have already suggested that the freedom of the individual is limited by the marketplace in subtle ways that Friedman and his like-minded colleagues overlook. Still, we must admit once again that there is *some* truth in what Friedman says here; and if we wish to defend a national health service on redistributive grounds, we should admit that there is an element of paternalism in so doing. If we give benefits to the poor in services rather than cash, it is at least partly because we believe that they will be better off with the services; and that even if they were able to buy adequate medical services with the money we gave them, some at least would spend it less prudently, so as to gain short-term satisfactions at a cost of greater distress and suffering in the long run.

Friedman (1962) grants that a paternalist position is internally consistent, but he associates it with dictatorship and insists that "those who believe in freedom must believe also in the freedom of individuals to make their own mistakes" (pp. 187–188). Paternalism, Friedman says, is an arrogant position, while the liberal displays humility in refusing to decide for others what is good for them. The standpoint from which Friedman criticizes paternalism, however, is the same superficial liberalism we encountered earlier. Friedman does not inquire into the social conditions and circumstances in which the poor decide how to spend their money. He does not consider the effect of being brought up in a family that never had the habit of providing for the future because there was never more than enough to provide for the present. He does not consider that alcoholism, drug addiction, or gambling may be factors in producing poverty. Is the alcoholic free to choose whether to invest his money in health insurance? He is not, and there are many others who may not be alcoholics but who, for a variety of reasons, are scarcely more able to make an informed, carefully considered, longterm choice. How often do we have to watch people do something they come to regret bitterly when it is too late to do anything about it, before we can say to the next person about to do the same thing that he is making a mistake? Is it really arrogant to claim that we may sometimes know what is in another person's interests better than he does himself? Or is it merely an honest appreciation of a fact that stares us in the face, a fact that could hardly be denied were it not for a prevailing mythology that demands that we do deny it.

The final justification I shall mention for overriding the freedom of each to spend his income as he prefers is one that relates to a theme that has run through this chapter: the nature of the community we live in. Here we must consider whether it is not desirable that a community be integrated in certain fundamental areas of life, rather than being divided along lines of class or race. As Brian Barry (1965, chap. 7) has noted, the promotion of this value distinguishes a national health service from a system of universal insurance that provides standard sums of money for given treatments, while leaving doctors and hospitals to charge what they will and the patient to make up the difference if he selects a doctor or hospital that charges above the standard amount. This insurance system would provide a basic level of care for everyone. I do not agree with Barry that this value is the *only* one that distinguishes these two systems of providing health care (I have suggested others in the course of this chapter); but it is true that universal insurance would provide many of the benefits of a national health service, including redistribution and the provision of security for all against the threat of ruinous expenditure on medical care. What the insurance proposal could not do, however, is provide an integrated health service that would be used by people of all classes and races. We would still have one standard of care for the wealthy and another for the poor.

How important is integration in the area of medicine? It does not seem to be as important as in education, for it does not determine a person's opportunities for the whole of his life to the extent that education does (although medicine may do this in exceptional cases). Still, there are important reasons for desiring integration in medicine too. As Barry (1965) says, "so long as those with money can buy exemption from the common lot the rulers and the generally dominant groups in a society will have little motive for making sure that the public facilities are of good quality" (p. 134). In other words, if we want good public facilities, we have to ensure that those who can complain effectively when standards are allowed to drop, use the facilities.

A more fundamental aspect of integration is that it makes a substantial difference to our image of our community. The knowledge that we are all in it together when it comes to vital things like medical care, and that your money cannot buy you anything that I am not equally entitled to, may do a good deal to mitigate the effects of inequality in other, less vital areas and create the atmosphere of community concern for all that I have already discussed.

This last consideration is the first one we have encountered that goes beyond even what the British National Health Service has achieved. Private medicine does exist in Britain, and very wealthy people do sometimes get treatments that the National Health Service does not provide. Money may allow one person to go down to London and be operated on by an outstanding surgeon, while another who could not afford this would have to accept the general level of surgery in the area in which he lived. Yet this is not a major problem. Because of the generally high standard of treatment that the National Health Service provides at no cost, and the high costs of private medicine, only a very few people avail themselves of private treatment. Of those who do, by no means all actually do receive treatment that is superior to that offered by the National Health Service. As long as private medicine remains such a minor part of health care as a whole, there seems to be no need to prohibit it altogether. Allowing private medicine to exist, can, as Barry suggests, be seen as a reasonable compromise between the values of freedom and integration.

NOTES

1. I did not fully recognize this incompatibility in Singer (1973).

2. A summary of some experiments that lead to this conclusion may be found in Wright (1971, pp. 133–139). Arrow (1972) writes of the risk that we will "use up recklessly the scarce resources of altruistic motivation," but he offers no support whatsoever for the view that altruism is, like oil, a commodity of which the more we use, the less we have.

3. Titmuss noted also that the introduction of "major medical expense insurance" in the United States did apparently lead to an increase in demand for treatment.

REFERENCES

Arrow, K. (1963) "Uncertainty and the Welfare Economics of Medical Care," *American Economic Review,* 53, 941–973.

Arrow, K. (1972) "Gifts and Exchanges," *Philosophy and Public Affairs,* 1, 343–362.

Barry, B. (1965) *Political Argument.* New York: The Humanities Press, chap. 7.

Friedman, M. (1962) *Capitalism and Freedom.* Chicago: University of Chicago Press.

Hayek, F. A. (1960) *Constitution of Liberty.* Chicago: University of Chicago Press.

Marx, K. (1844/1967) *The Economic and Philosophic Manuscripts of 1844* (trans. by M. Milligan), D. J. Strink, ed. New York: International Publishers.

Marx, K. (1875/1938) *Critique of the Gotha Program.* New York: International Publishers.

Medical Malpractice: The Patient versus the Physician. (1969) Report of the Senate Subcommittee on Executive Reorganization and Government Research, Washington, D.C.

National Times (Sydney, Australia), April 4, 1977.

New York Times, January 8, 1974.

Report of the Secretary's Commission on Medical Malpractice. (1973) Washington, D.C.: Department of Health, Education, and Welfare.

Ribicoff, A. (1972) *The American Medical Machine.* New York: Harrow Books.

Singer, P. (1973) "Altruism and Commerce: A Defense of Titmuss against Arrow," *Philosophy and Public Affairs,* 2, 312–320.

Titmuss, R. M. (1963) *Essays on "The Welfare State."* London: Unwin University Books.

Titmuss, R. M. (1968) *Commitment to Welfare.* New York: Pantheon Books.

Titmuss, R. M. (1970) *The Gift Relationship.* London: Allen and Unwin.

Village Voice, February 21, 1974.

Wright, D. (1971) *The Psychology of Moral Behavior.* London: Penguin Books.

10

DIFFICULTIES IN THE ECONOMIC
ANALYSIS OF RIGHTS

CHARLES FRIED
Harvard Law School

The exaggerated claims that economic analysis in general and the market model in particular provide the key to the science of morals (to paraphrase John Austin's phrase) are obviously preposterous.[1] One would have thought that the sustained barrage of objections to the coherence and empirical soundness of such views, since Bentham (1780/1970) put forward his moral calculus, would have had its effect by now. That these objections have not had much inhibiting effect outside of

The material in this chapter is drawn from an early version of a larger work, *Right and Wrong*, now in press. My views have changed over the intervening years. This work began in 1971 with the assistance of a grant from the John Simon Guggenheim Foundation. Versions of this chapter were presented to the Seminaire Walras at the École Pratique des Hautes Études of the University of Paris, and to the Society for Ethical and Legal Philosophy in 1972. In addition to the suggestions I have received from members of the groups to whom I have presented earlier versions of this paper, I am particularly grateful for the kind assistance of Serge-Christophe Kolm and Christian Schmidt.

academic moral theory is itself an interesting chapter in the sociology of knowledge. The latter day adherents of the moral calculus might perhaps find the situation quite natural, emphasizing as they do the differences between their position and Bentham's rather crude hedonism. But the differences are not nearly as great as they imagine. Indeed, one might say that what has been gained since the days of the classical utilitarians in invulnerability to obvious empirical objections has been purchased only at the price of increasing emptiness of the theory. As one economist, commenting on the currently voguish view of rights growing out of the work of Ronald Coase, has put it, there is almost no distance between the conclusions and the premises. Certainly the brilliant formal complexity with which some of the analyses in this mode are characterized accounts for much of its continued fascination. So, I suspect, and less flatteringly, does the fact that the practitioners of this mode of analysis tend to be relatively ignorant of arguments and traditions outside their own disciplines. They persist in the face of philosophical refutations that are unknown to them. For these reasons, one feels a certain diffidence in launching into this subject yet another time. Nevertheless, that diffidence should not be mistaken for timidity. It is not that one doubts that the job can be done, but rather that one wonders why it has to be done.

In this chapter, rather than review the familiar (but not for that reason less valid) general objections, I shall focus on the concept of rights, and more specifically apply it to the notion of health as a right. In the first part of the chapter, I will review the currently fashionable view of rights propagated by such writers as Coase (1960), Demsetz (1957, 1964, 1966), Calabresi (1970), and Posner (1973) and will offer some criticisms. I will then apply those criticisms to the area of health as an example of how alternative and more morally plausible ways of thinking would proceed.

THE ECONOMIC ANALYSIS—A CRITIQUE

Bargaining and Moral Foundations

The general concept of rights[2] in law and morals is important to my critique of the economic model of social analysis because rights represent the starting points from which bargaining takes place, the counters that are exchanged in bargaining, and the rules or constraints under which bargaining goes forward. Whether my false teeth or my blood are my property (Fried, 1970, 1974; Williams, 1962, p. 125)—i.e., whether I have rights in them—will determine whether in bargaining I must pay to keep them or others must pay to get them. Whether fraud and force are to be admitted as techniques of bargaining, and indeed whether bargains themselves will be enforced, also crucially determine what the net effect of the bargaining process will be.[3] All these determinants or constraints can be viewed as permanent, secure rights.

For a time, these problems and their implications for the economic analysis of social welfare were overlooked. It seemed to go without saying that the person who takes affirmative action, who imposes on others, who disturbs the status quo is the one who must purchase the right to do so (Mishan, 1967). The person in passive possession of this or that right was obviously the one whose cooperation had to be suborned. It is the great virtue of writers such as Ronald Coase and those who have followed him to have noticed the radical reciprocity in all these situations: the homemaker who hangs her laundry may be thought of as imposing on the soot-producing factory just as much as the factory imposes on her; deception in bargaining relates simply to having and communicating knowledge, and knowledge, of course, is a prime subject for bargaining or economic exchange; and violence is a term of opprobrium, but in fact freedom from physical imposition is something that can be purchased, as—reciprocally—can be the right to impose physically. Moreover, the mechanisms of justice by which contracts are enforced can be seen as goods that we may or may not wish to procure. Finally, in this view, the capacity to bind oneself or others simply provides a further strategic advantage or counter in dealing in a bargaining situation (Schelling, 1960, 1968, 1973).

Why, then, do we have such strong ethical intuitions about these matters? Why do we believe that intentional bodily harm, deception, and the breaking of promises are wrong? Why do we believe that correlative with this sense of wrong are rights to security, property, honesty, and perhaps to goods such as medical care or subsistence levels of clothing and housing? The analysts I am considering point out that in a frictionless world, free of bargaining costs, an efficient result must occur, irrespective of whether, say, rapists or their victims must pay for the right to have their way.[4] (The conclusion, at first surprising, should not be. It follows immediately on the definition of efficiency: the outcome of bargaining by rational agents in a world free of transaction costs.) How do we account, then, for these strongly held, persistent intuitions of right? The argument would have it that in our real world in which not all bargains are free of cost, imperfections will be corrected and bargaining is more likely to attain efficiency if one, rather than the other, point of departure obtains. If the bargain could really be struck and enforced without cost, the use of land for planting crops or the exploitation of hunting grounds would be optimal. But since some bargains are more costly than others, efficient solutions are more likely to be attained if farmers are given property rights in the fields they cultivate or tribes are given exlusive rights to trap fur-bearing animals in particular territories.[5] But the basis of such rights is no more fundamental or intrinsic than that.

These theories push the economic analysis to further, more startling limits. Rather than representing a structure built upon a foundation of common-sense ethical presuppositions, these more recent inquiries purport to supplant, explain, and thus call into question that foundation of common sense. Indeed, for the first time in a radical way, the market is proposed as the fundamental mode for morals. To put the point differently, as long as moral institutions or tradition accorded us our rights and defined the limits of bargaining, the pretensions of the market model were limited, harmless, and perhaps useful. But by this new critique, the market model seeks to replace or provide the analysis of that moral foundation.

Unfortunately, this critique is too radical. If the morality of bargaining is itself to be the subject of bargaining, then one must still ask under what constraints this second-order bargaining is to take place. Indeed, to the extent that force, fraud, and the honoring of bargains are themselves seen as the subject of bargaining, the model necessarily loses any normative power and becomes at best a purely descriptive model. It becomes a model of how "rational" people do in fact behave, but it loses any semblance of plausibility as an account of how they should behave. Of course, this may reveal a fundamental misunderstanding by these analysts of the nature of ethics. Ethics is certainly not a description of behavior, not even a description of "rational" behavior, and not even the description of the "rationality" of behavior that some people consider ethical. By contrast, if we have a firm theory of rights (both property rights defining what is ours to bargain with, and procedural rights setting forth the acceptable modes of bargaining), then it is plausible—perhaps more than plausible—that the bargaining procedures built up on a moral foundation will have significant moral content.

Distribution

One repeated, standard response to this criticism is the introduction of distribution as a further factor in the analysis. Before I show how this factor is included in the analysis of rights, a distinction must be made between two kinds of distributive ethical judgments—those that accept the premise of consumer sovereignty and those that do not.[6] Those that do not are judgments that would override the operation of the market, not in the name of realizing individual preferences as they actually are, but out of some sense that certain results are good in spite of or in addition to those preferences. If a solution nobody wanted were imposed on the grounds that it was "good," this would be anti-individualistic. These forms of judgment would extend further. The solution that is adopted may happen to be the preference of some portion of the relevant group; the result is still anti-individualistic if it is adopted, not on the basis of realizing the preferences of the members of the groups (conflicts being determined in terms of either number or intensity), but rather by some judgment as to the intrinsic value of those preferences. This form of judgment shades over into paternalism when the adoption of a solution is based, not on any judgment that a certain state of affairs is better irrespective of whether it serves the interests of the individual members of the groups, but rather on the supposition that it does indeed serve the interests of some or all of those members, but they do not know it.

Consumer sovereignty criteria determine the distribution of

satisfaction (welfare) or scarce resources within the group by one of a class of rules expressed, not in terms of the intrinsic value of the satisfaction, but rather in terms of the value of the persons whose interests are realized. The most familiar example of such a distributive norm is equality, which posits the equal value of all members of the group and makes no judgment as to the things that the individuals prefer, only that each has an equal right to have whatever it is that he or she prefers.

Distributive judgments are admitted to be normative, ethical, and (it is usually added in the literature) subjective. It is generally recognized that such distributional judgments are inevitable. Even to accept the status quo and not to make judgments is implicitly to make a normative judgment that the status quo represents an ethically tolerable point of departure, or at least one that one is not ethically entitled to change. But what is done with this concession to ethics is in fact entirely unsatisfactory.

Distribution, Efficiency, and Rights

The model (greatly simplified) takes the following form: ethical judgments relate to distribution, while the function of the market in bargaining is allocative efficiency. As I have indicated, the analysis would have it that in an ideal, frictionless world, the free market would be allowed to operate without impediment. In our actual friction-fraught world, rights are assigned so as to approximate as closely as possible the workings of a frictionless market (Calabresi, 1970; Coase, 1960; Demsetz, 1957, 1964, 1966; and Polinsky, 1974). Since it is recognized that how rights are assigned (i.e., what the starting point for bargaining and the constraints on it are to be) makes a difference to distribution and to the relative welfare of individuals, the outcome is adjusted to accord with our ethical, distributive norm by a separate process of lump sum transfers that is effected outside of the market bargaining process. Once again, any systematic connection between rights and ethics is denied.

One might put the matter this way: according to the modern economic analysis of rights, the only right of an individual that is independent of the contingencies of what is needed to attain efficiency in that particular state of affairs (one might say the only moral or pre-economic right one has) is the right to whatever distributional share of the efficient total our ethical norm assigns to that person. But there are no rights in particular, concrete goods—at least not pre-economic or moral rights.

It is well known that it is difficult, if not impossible, to design mechanisms for lump sum transfers that do not interfere with efficiency, for instance by distorting incentives and thus leading to a suboptimal allocation between leisure and work (Samuelson, 1947), but I shall ignore these difficulties. My criticism is of a different order: I maintain that a large—and it seems to me better—class of social welfare distributive criteria determines the distribution of at least some rights directly. If this is so, then in respect to those criteria and those rights, at least it is not a question of defining rights so as to obtain efficiency, with distributional adjustments being made by lump sum transfers that leave the allocation of rights unchanged. In other words, in respect to some aspects of social welfare, the criterion and currency is the enjoyment of certain rights as such. And although economic analysis can tell us what might be the effect on allocation of recognizing these rights, it cannot pretend to provide the means for deriving these rights from economic premises.

Absolute Preferences

The economic analysis is intuitively unappealing, insofar as it suggests that all rights, even such basic rights as liberty of conscience, political rights, or the right to be free of deliberate physical incursions, are themselves not moral rights but contingent derivations of an optimizing mechanism. In any case, where the individuals concerned have systems of preferences that cannot be said to describe a utility function, for instance wherever an individual would prefer a certain good absolutely over some or all other goods, then there may be no other way to assure him his morally entitled distributive share without according him only that good. Or, to put the matter differently, if individuals have lexicographically[7] ordered individual values, then the only lump sum redistribution that would assure them their distributive shares would simply be whatever distribution would allow them to purchase the very goods that might have been taken away from them under the efficiency leg of the argument.

Now this difficulty not only undermines the economic analysis of rights, but also argues for a wholly indeterminate situation if these "poorly behaved" preference functions are also different for different persons. In such a case, we may be unable to maintain our distributional commitment to some of the members of the society. In other words, we had all better agree in respect to these fiercely held preferences, or if we do not agree, then the only way to account for the solution we arrive at is by putting forward ethical norms that do not pretend to seek merely the aggregation of actual preferences. For our ethical norm as to what is the correct distribution of welfare will have to permit the overriding of the preferences of some discordant members of the society without any notion that this can be made up to them by any lump sum transfer. Once we assume that individuals can have what I call "absolute preferences," then any concern for their welfare must treat the realization of these preferences as rights, and we must free ourselves from the notion that there is only one moral right to one's distributive share. The reason is that the distributive share can be dealt out only by what I might call the "material recognition of the rights." Later in this chapter, I shall argue that it is plausible to consider certain interests in health as having for the individual this kind of status, and thus compelling this kind of material recognition.

Needs[8]

A further difficulty with the economic analysis of rights relates to the way in which the welfare that is distributionally required shall be measured: subjectively (in terms of money) or some other objective index. An objective index is acceptable only if we are prepared to assume either that such objective goods lead to the same level of welfare in all individuals, or if we have as part of our distributional norm the notion that the subjective welfare derived from objective resources is not a matter of normative concern. To some extent we do believe one or both of these things. Where basic needs have been met, we are prepared to say that it is fair to give people with expensive tastes and cheap tastes the same amount of money. Or, alternatively, if people (always assuming basic needs have been met) are somehow unhappy even though they have received their fair share of money, goods, or whatever, we say that this is not the concern of social ethics. But these positions are tolerable only if basic needs are met. If, however, an individual requires a large amount of money simply to maintain his health, there seems to be something wrong with a view that says that the reasonable distributive norm is one that gives him the same amount of money (if equality is our distributive norm) as everyone else, even though he must live at little more than a subsistence level after he has purchased the medicines he needs just to remain alive. A need for medicine stands on a different footing from a desire for caviar, race horses, or champagne, and people should not be allowed to change the status of luxury desires by arguing that these things represent as much a necessity to them as medicine represents to the dying. In short, our distributive norm cannot afford to be measured either wholly by the objective share of goods, or wholly subjectively in terms of what those goods represent to the recipient. Instead, we must have a theory that identifies certain preferences or values as what I shall call needs, so that welfare in respect to these is measured by the result for the individual. The individual cannot be allowed to determine for himself what will be placed in this category, nor can a person decide what constitutes the correct index of results. Once again I shall argue that health is an interest that must appropriately be placed in the category of needs, and the distribution of resources toward health must be determined by different criteria than the distribution of what I would call "elective goods."

Preferences Are Not Brute Facts

The economic analysis of rights, particularly as it relates to such areas as health, is inadequate for reasons of a different sort. The economic analysis, and the criticisms I have been making of it so far, takes preferences, values, and needs as given and sets itself the task of rationalizing them in a world of scarce resources and conflicting claims. Now one can proceed in the way on one of two assumptions: (1) that preferences, values, and needs are brute facts about which nothing more can be said, so that they must form the primitive data of the system; or (2) that there are moral reasons why society should take values, preferences, and needs as given, rather than going behind them in imposing social solutions. Although many working in the economic mode may believe the first assumption to be true, no reason for this belief is provided. If the argument shifts to the second assumption, philosophers and theorists are not precluded from discussing with each individual, on a personal basis, how he should preceive his values, preferences, and needs, even though for reasons of principle we leave him the last word when it comes to formulating a social rule.

Indeed, philosophy has traditionally engaged in that second enterprise, and as we think about markets and morals in general, and markets for things like health care in particular, we might ask whether the commitment to leaving the consumer the last word in the public arena has not obscured from philosophers (in the broad sense) the educational and philosophical task of debating with individuals about what their values should be as they enter the marketplace.

I would go even further. Not only must we be prepared to dispute with the individual "consumer" his system of preferences, but we must be willing to impose upon him "paternalistically" at least to this extent: We must recognize that the very concept of choice or preference, as it is used in an argument that social morality requires consumer sovereignty, presupposes a certain rationality, a certain stability, a certain degree of contact with reality on the part of the consumer. Otherwise, what we have cannot even be described as choice or as a system of preferences, but only as random behavior. If the consumer sovereignty model, and the market model built upon it, are to serve anything other than descriptive purposes, there must be some reason to think that the behavior entered into the model is something more than random behavior. Even when such a model is used to analyze bizarre and seemingly irrational behavior, its usefulness as a heuristic device resides only in the assumption that the behavior in question has a purpose and rationality after all. And when it is put forward as a normative tool, surely some stringency may be admitted in what will be allowed to count as a choice system.

THE SELF AS THE UNIT OF CHOICE

The Self as Substance: Identity and Continuity

In this section, I shall put together the critique I have offered of the economic analysis of rights, seeking to show how a more adequate conception emerges from it. All three objections—that some values or preferences cannot be smoothly traded off or compensated for by other values and preferences of the individual, that a sensible normative rule must take into account needs as measured by objective criteria, and that the very concept of preference structure implies some constraints on what should count as a preference structure—might all be seen as converging on the notion that any acceptable, normative scheme must build on a theory of the self. That is, our notion of choosing individuals cannot be a notion of persons as normatively dimensionless points without characteristics (like Lockeian substances), tastes, needs, and physical characteristics being ascribed merely as parameters in an equation that will determine what the level of satisfaction enjoyed by that "self" will be.[9]

Although I do not feel able to give either a formal or an elaborate account of the conception of a self that I have in mind, certain aspects seem important and relate to the three objections I have detailed in the first section. The most formal of the characteristics defining a self have to do with its identity and continuity. The kinds of entities to whom values, preferences, choices, and the realization of these can be attributed are human bodies that persist over time, the continuity of which is the continuity of the self. Thus, an entity that existed only momentarily, or indeed for a period of time shorter than that of the living body with which it is associated, would not form a recognizable unit for the ascription of our concepts. The idea, for instance, that four or more "selves" inhabit the same persistent living body, would be so problematical that our ethics would not know what to do with it. I suppose we would have an analogous difficulty with the claim that a single self is to be associated with more than one living body, either simultaneously or sequentially, as in some notion of the transmigration of souls.[10]

This relatively formal notion can be fleshed out by the introduction of certain, more contingent psychological assumptions regarding the persistence and unity of the self. I shall not go into these in detail, but I would say that those psychological laws that bear on the conditions necessary first for the development and then for the maintenance of a firm, consistent, and unitary concept of the self, must also stand as the basis for any ethical judgments regarding the satisfactions of such a self. It should not be taken for granted that such a concept of the self always has and must necessarily develop as a matter of fact along with a persistent human body. Radical departures from this usual course of development tend to be viewed as some kind of insanity or monstrosity. But such departures only prove that the development of such a concept of self requires the existence of certain conditions, a certain nurturance, and a certain reinforcement.

Conditions for the Realization of a Sense of Self

Moving one step further, but still from a purely formal notion of self, I would incorporate in my argument the concept of self-respect as developed by Rawls (1971, chap. 7). For present purposes, it is sufficient to recall that Rawls gives as one of the most important of his "primary goods" the good of self-respect, which is the providing of that system of support to an individual that is necessary for his belief in the worth and seriousness of his system of values and preferences. Two aspects of this account should be emphasized here. First, that the good of self-respect is not—like other goods, or even other primary goods—a material condition for the realization of this or that particular end or desire. Rather, it is a set of background conditions that establishes the whole system of an individual's ends and desires as significant. Second, self-respect is a radically relational and systematic kind of good, in that its realization consists of the adherence by others to certain principles of action. It cannot be provided to the indidivual just by giving him this or that thing. It requires that others treat him as an individual worthy of respect. And this requires a system of attitudes and actions to exemplify those attitudes.

These aspects of the concept of the self relate to the three objections to the economic analysis of rights. There are material conditions for the development and maintenance of the integrity of the self, just as there are material conditions for the maintenance of self-respect. Given the priority of the concept of self, it should not be surprising that the interest in those material conditions is of a wholly different order from the interest in other conditions for the realization of other goods. It should not be surprising that these conditions should be given the absolute status, which, however, destroys the workability of the economic analysis of rights. Moreover, the assertion of such an absolute priority does not entail the radical incoherence of social norms that I have said would result if some or all members of the society had preference structures containing such absolute priorities, with no convergence across individuals. The concept of the self being a general philosophical concept, it is reasonable to assume convergence among individuals of the material conditions necessary for the realization of each of their selves.

Further, the exigencies of the concept of self entail a social norm defined in terms of needs, objectively identified, rather than in terms either of objective goods irrespective of needs or of subjective satisfactions. What is needed is the fulfillment in each individual's circumstances of the preconditions of a coherent concept of self. As the circumstances of the individual vary, so will the material needed to satisfy those conditions vary; and thus the norm must be specified in terms of needs. On the other hand, the concept of self is philosophical and objective, and what constitutes the satisfaction of this need is properly the subject of objective inquiry.

Finally, it should be readily apparent how my last objection to the economic analysis of rights relates to the conception of the self I have sketched. If a satisfactory analysis of welfare based on preference and choice must assume the coherence and rationality of the preference structure, then this involves importing into the analysis whatever conditions emerge from the development of a theory of the self. For it is a self that has preference structures and systems of value. Only those things will count as choices or preferences that can be ascribed to entitites meeting the substantive conditions of self, and the concept of a system of preferences will itself relate to the systematizing elements within such a conception of self.

Let me be explicit as to why these constraints and conditions imposed on the marked model lead to a system of fundamental rights. Whatever interests are established or whatever limits on bargaining are imposed, can be seen as establishing rights in respect to those interests and limits. And since they logically precede the bargaining model, such rights do not depend on the contingencies of the outcome of the model once put into operation. If the theory of the self yields the conclusion that necessary to the integrity of the self is a firm sense that one's body is one's own and not social property, then it follows that bargaining must proceed from the starting point that our bodies are our own. And that is what I mean by a fundamental or pre-economic right.

THE CASE OF HEALTH

Material and Residual Rights

The right to health is not one of the categorical, negative rights such as are handed down in the Ten Commandments. The prohibitions against murder, theft, and deception, for instance, together with the correlative rights they imply, might be thought of as existing extrasocially; if there had ever been a state of nature, these rights and duties would have been present within it. The right to a particular distributive share is a paradigm of a right that requires a social context, an institutional context. Political rights provide another set of paradigms. The right to health, if it exists at all, is plainly a social, institutional right. The interest in the case of the right to health is that it presents an example of an institutional right, which is neither political nor a contingent derivation from whatever distributive share this society's social welfare function recognizes as the particular individual's right. My claim will be that a social welfare function that speaks, say, of an equal distribution or of a maximum distribution must be taken to refer essentially to residual goods.

Residual goods are the vast collection of things people want and from which they derive welfare, which are left over after essential needs have been supplied. It is my notion that health, education, food, housing, clothing, as well as access to the political and adjudicatory processes of the society, are all essential needs, which should not come under the terms of the social welfare function.[11] Rather, the social welfare function should govern the distribution of the vast, heterogeneous range of goods that people want once their essential needs have been satisfied.

In proposing such a dichotomy, I do not mean to suggest that these residual goods are somehow trivial or unworthy. They are residual in the sense that no material argument regarding their status of rights directly (rather than through the exercise of market power determined by the distributive share) can be put forward. No doubt the arguments for the derivation of a material right to, say, political participation or education show as well that there is a certain priority, a certain basic quality to such a right. But I do not wish to overstate this point of priority. After all, in any decent society these rights can generally be taken for granted so that the burden of economic and political concern will relate to the realization of the residual goods. These residual goods might be thought of as being those goods that free people in a situation of relative prosperity seek in the realization of their freedom. And there is nothing second-rate about that. If these material rights are taken as basic, let us be sure precisely what this status means. It is like saying, perhaps, that absence of deep political corruption is basic to a good society. It is basic only in the sense that in the presence of such corruption other social and political goods are insecure. Yet for that very reason, we hesitate to define a good society in terms of the presence or absence of political corruption. Rather, we would like to assume this absence, and then go on to other things.

Respecting an Embodied Self

The argument that the right to health is basic in this sense depends on our ability to show that health (or some aspects of it) have the quality of being necessary preconditions for the general enjoyment of a just distributive share. Though I shall not attempt to make that argument in detail, the concept of the self put forward in the second section provides the foundations for the argument. It is critical that the self is an embodied self. An individual cannot, consistently with the concept of the integrity of an embodied self, treat his body or its needs as an entity separate from himself, to which he can—if he chooses—allocate resources, provided that his preference structure dictates this as the most efficient use of those resources. For such a view of the body would imply that the self is one thing and the body another, having no more than a contingent or instrumental relation to the self. This is not to say that a person may not rationally encounter physical dangers, for instance. My point is only that, in endangering his body, he endangers himself—that there is no way to endanger one without endangering the other.

If the self is an embodied self, then it follows that some aspects at least of care for that physical substrate of the self are essential to the integrity of the self. Plainly, that interest is not absolute; rational people at all times have assumed the right, and have been thought to have the right, to endanger that physical integrity in the pursuit of one or another interest—including riches. The only point is that, in using up the body, man uses up himself.

Health and the Integrity of Self

This shows both the sense in which health relates to generalized welfare or residual goods and the sense in which it might be viewed as providing the foundation for both the self and its pursuits. In this dual nature it differs from, let us say, the basic goods of self-respect or liberty. For we do not think that we use these up in the pursuit of our other goals, but rather we just use them. Evidently, both the psychology and the philosophy of health is complex and elusive. Perhaps, after all, we do not use up our health in the pursuit of our goods so much as we use it in much the same way as we use our liberty in choosing one of two ends, both of which we are free to choose.

In any event, the foundational aspect of the right to health is better seen not so much in its absolute priority to other goods—for I suspect we would have a hard time establishing this in any thoroughgoing way—but rather by our natural tendency to treat it as a need and not as a good. That is, I am inclined to suggest that just distributional schemes would not (if equality were our canon of just distribution) be satisfied by an equal distribution of money with which the chronically ill could purchase medicines while others purchased holidays, opera tickets, or other luxury goods. Good health is a need precisely in the sense that we have or we seek objective measures of good health. We try to assure this objective good, the satisfaction of this objective need apart from, or without prejudice to, the balance of an individual's distributive share. That we treat health in this way is precisely indicative of the status we accord it. It is in this sense that it may appropriately be considered a right.

There are very great complexities in working out the details of this notion. Plainly, we are prepared to do things as a society that will irremediably endanger the health of some of our citizens—environmental hazards offer the obvious example. Moreover, we are not willing to do everything we can to restore the health of those who are disadvantaged in this respect. Not only are we unwilling to make available the necessary resources to provide what is presently within our ability for all members of our society, but we also refrain from taking those steps that are likely to increase our capacities in the future. Finally, we are miles away from any notion that we should try to "compensate" those whose sufferings are beyond medical help. We are far from thinking that the hopelessly mentally retarded, the aged, and the mentally ill should be treated as the most favored members of the society, since in respect to a fundamental good (their health) they are doomed beyond hope. Which of these tendencies represents the true moral intuition of our society? Or, is there a way in which the two can be reconciled? My guess is that any analysis departing from acceptable moral principles will show that we do far too little for the chronically unfortunate, while perhaps we do too much to overcome the effects of some illnesses, those being the very illnesses that in the end must strike everybody. My guess would be that a truly just allocation in this respect would move away from those illnesses that will eventually kill us all and toward those that make an unfortunate minority miserable throughout their lifetimes. The reason seems quite clear. Those illnesses that are sufficiently widespread that people may think contracting them is probable, are precisely those illnesses that it is fair and reasonable for us to accept philosophically, and about which it is fair to say that we would rather spend our resources in pursuing other goods and take our chances with, for example, cancer and heart disease. But where the disease strikes at birth, during youth, or in some other way "out of season," then we have a special obligation because the victims of such diseases cannot be seen as having participated in the benefits of a societal choice to enrich life in other ways. Ironically, the same lack of community identification with such unfortunates is precisely what leads us to relegate them to the worst categories of care.[12]

NOTES

1. The immediate progenitor of this claim, as of the notion of utility in general, is, of course, Bentham (1970). This is not to say that the "felicific calculus" does not have significant roots in earlier philosophical writing, even among the Greeks. The tradition of what might be called the free market liberals, such as von Mises, Hayek, and Friedman continue this tradition, prescinding, however, from the Benthamic premises regarding the comparability and additivity of individual utilities. As the work of modern-day Benthamites such as Harsanyi (1955) shows, this is a less radical departure from classical utilitarian principles than might be thought. A most sophisticated form of utilitarianism as an analysis of social ethics arose out of game theory. For recent, lucid examples, see Schelling (1968, 1973). For two extreme and enthusiastic examples of the application of market theory to social policy, see Posner (1973) and Tullock (1971).

2. For a recent, excellent exposition of the concept of rights that I am assuming, see Dworkin (1977, chaps. 6 and 7) and Fried (1974).

3. On this point, both Posner (1973) and Tullock (1971) are explicit.

4. It has been suggested by Professor George Fletcher that the Coase theorem should not be applied to cases of intentional impositions but only to "externalities"—that is to say, unintended impositions incidental to the pursuit of some other end. Although many of the initial examples used by Coase (1960) and Demsetz (1957, 1964, 1966) are of this latter sort, and indeed the Coase theorem was devised to deal with the traditional problem of externalities, there is nothing in the theorem itself that would limit it in this way. Moreover, it is the very point of the analysis that the distinction between intended impositions and side effects or externalities cannot be analytically maintained. This is clearly seen in Posner's (1973) and

Tullock's (1971) application of it. If bargaining in the absence of transaction costs would produce efficiency in respect to unintended impositions—ordinary externalities—then what is there in the theory that prevents the same conclusion being reached in respect to intended impositions? That this might be seen as a *reductio ad absurdum* of the Coase theorem is hardly an argument against the *reductio* itself, but rather against the theorem.

5. These examples are drawn from Demsetz (1957, 1964, 1966).

6. For two excellent introductions to these subjects, see Graaff (1957) and Sen (1970).

7. Values *a, b, c, . . . n* are said to be ordered lexicographically when all *a*'s are preferred to any *b*'s, all *b*'s to any *c*'s, all *i*'s to any *j*'s. Thus, in a dictionary, words are ordered lexicographically. An index number is not assigned to each letter in the word and a weighted average taken. Instead, the words are arranged by their initial letters, and then by their second letters, and so on. For a full discussion of lexicographical orderings and their significance in moral theory, see Rawls (1971), Banerjec (1964), and Sen (1970).

8. In my forthcoming work, *Right and Wrong*, I take a substantially different position on the matter in this and the last section of the present essay.

9. It would seem that, in the view I have just characterized, a self would in principle choose not only the realization of whatever preferences it happened to have, but also those preferences that, in the world as it is, promised the highest degree of realization. Indeed, even if for some reason the self would not or could not choose its preferences in this way, this theory would provide no basis for objecting if others imposed, not limits on realizations of actual preferences, but the preferences themselves, as long as the degree of satisfaction or "utility," however measured by the distributive norm, was higher than that attainable under the actual preferences of that self. Nor is it open to such analysts to argue that it is just part of the distributive norm or social welfare function, that no action be taken to alter (fundamentally?) the self's system of preferences. Why should this be part of the distributive norm? What is "distributive" about such a constraint? Surely, to import this constraint into the social welfare function is to do precisely what I am arguing for, i.e., to constrain our whole mode of argumentation by a material notion of the self. Finally, this objection does not entail an infinite regress: one can wish to be happy without wishing for the only things available to make one happy.

10. For further development of these notions, see Fried (1970, chap. 11; 1974).

11. See Arrow (1963) and Fried (1974). Michelman (1973) is a detailed and important argument for the general proposition that the kinds of basic needs discussed here constitute not only moral rights but constitutionally protected rights as well.

12. It might be argued that the institution of the medical deduction in the federal income tax represents a recognition of some of these notions:

medical expenditures are deductible on the theory that they are non-optional and based on needs, not wants. Moreover, they are deductible only as they exceed 3 percent of income, in recognition of the fact that some medical expenses—like food or clothing—are general to all, and that it is only the excess that represents unusual needs. For a full examination of these views, see Andrews (1972).

REFERENCES

Andrews, W. (1972) "Personal Deductions in an Ideal Income Tax," *Harvard Law Review*, 86, p. 309.

Arrow, K. (1963) "Uncertainty and the Welfare Economics of Medical Care," *American Economic Review*, 53, p. 941.

Banerjee, D. (1964) "Choice and Order: Or First Things First," *Economica*, (n.s. 158) 31, p. 158.

Bentham, J. (1970) *An Introduction to the Principles of Morals and Legislation* (H. L. A. Hart, ed.). London: Athlone. (Originally published, 1780.)

Calabresi, G. (1970) *The Cost of Accidents.* New Haven, Conn.: Yale University Press.

Coase, R. (1960) "The Problem of Social Cost," *Journal of Law and Economics*, 3, p. 67.

Demsetz, H. (1957) "Towards a Theory of Property Rights," *American Economic Review* (No. 2, Papers and Proceedings), 57, p. 347.

Demsetz, H. (1964) "The Exchange and Enforcement of Property Rights," *Journal of Law and Economics*, 7, p. 11.

Demsetz, H. (1966) "Some Aspects of Property Rights," *Journal of Law and Economics*, 9, p. 61.

Dworkin, R. (1977) *Taking Rights Seriously.* Cambridge, Mass.: Harvard University Press.

Fried, C. (1970) *An Anatomy of Values.* Cambridge, Mass.: Harvard University Press.

Fried, C. (1974) *Human Experimentation: Personal Integrity and Social Policy.* Amsterdam: Elsevier.

Graaff, J. (1957) *Theoretical Welfare Economics.* Cambridge, England: Cambridge University Press.

Harsanyi, J. (1955) "Cardinal Welfare, Individualistic Ethics, and Interpersonal Comparisons of Utility," *Journal of Political Economy*, 63, p. 309.

Michelman, F. (1973) "In Pursuit of Constitutional Welfare Rights," *University of Pennsylvania Law Review*, 121, p. 962.

Mishan, E. (1967) "Pareto Optimality and the Law," *Oxford Economic Papers*, 19, p. 285.

Polinsky, M. (1974) "Economic Analysis as a Potentially Defective Product: A Buyer's Guide to Posner's Economic Analysis of Law," *Harvard Law Review*, 87, p. 1655.

Posner, R. (1973) *Economic Analysis of Law.* Boston: Little, Brown.

Rawls, J. (1971) *A Theory of Justice.* Cambridge, Mass.: Harvard University Press.

Samuelson, P. (1947) *Foundations of Economic Analysis.* Cambridge, Mass.: Harvard University Press.

Schelling, T. C. (1960) *The Strategy of Conflict.* Cambridge, Mass.: Harvard University Press.

Schelling, T. C. (1968) "Game Theory and the Study of Ethical Systems," *Journal of Conflict Resolution,* 12, p. 34.

Schelling, T. C. (1973) "Hockey Helmets, Concealed Weapons, and Daylight Saving," *Journal of Conflict Resolution,* 17, p. 381.

Sen, A. (1970) *Collective Choice and Social Welfare.* San Francisco: Holden-Day

Tullock, G. (1971) *The Logic of the Law.* New York: Basic.

Williams, B. (1962) "The Idea of Equality," in P. Laslett and W. Runciman, ed., *Philosophy, Politics and Society.* New York: Barnes & Noble.

CONFERENCE PARTICIPANTS

Professor Bernard Barber, Department of Sociology, Barnard College, New York, New York 10027

Professor James M. Buchanan, Department of Economics, Virginia Polytechnic Institute, Blacksburg, Virginia 23220

Dr. Samuel Calian, University of Dubuque, Theological Seminary, Dubuque, Iowa 52001

Professor Robert Coburn, Department of Philosophy, University of Washington, Seattle, Washington 98195

Dr. Gerald Cohen, Department of Philosophy, University College, University of London, London, England

Professor Meinolf Dierkes, Battelle-Institut e.V., 6000 Frankfurt/Main 90, Postschliessfach 900160, West Germany

Professor George Fletcher, School of Law, Harvard University, Cambridge, Massachusetts 02138

Professor Charles Fried, School of Law, Harvard University, Cambridge, Massachusetts 02138

Dr. Raymond Gastil, Battelle Seattle Research Center, 4000 N.E. 41st Street, Seattle, Washington 98105

Professor Harold Hochman, Graduate School of Public Policy, University of California, 2607 Hearst Avenue, Berkeley, California 94720

Professor John Junker, School of Law, University of Washington, Seattle, Washington 98195

Professor Reuben Kessel (*now deceased*), Graduate School of Business, University of Chicago.

Professor Edward E. Lawler, III, Institute for Social Research, University of Michigan, Ann Arbor, Michigan 48104

Professor Gerald Leventhal, Department of Psychology, Wayne State University, Detroit, Michigan 48202

Professor Kenneth McCaffree, Battelle Human Affairs Research Center, 4000 N.E. 41st Street, Seattle, Washington 98105

Dr. Charles L. Miller, Battelle Human Affairs Research Center, 4000 N.E. 41st Street, Seattle, Washington 98105

Professor Edward Nell, Department of Economics, 66th West 12th Street, New School of Social Research, New York, New York 10011

Dr. Douglas North, Chairman, Department of Economics, University of Washington, Seattle, Washington

Professor Edmund S. Phelps, Department of Economics, Columbia University, New York, New York 10027

Professor Robert Richman, Department of Philosophy, University of Washington, Seattle, Washington 98195

Professor Thomas Scanlon, Department of Philosophy, Princeton University, Princeton, New Jersey 08540

Professor Tibor Scitovsky, Department of Economics, University of British Columbia, Vancouver, British Columbia, Canada

Mr. Peter Singer, Department of Philosophy, Monash University, Clayton, Victoria, Australia

Professor Burkhard Strumpel, Institute for Social Research, University of Michigan, Ann Arbor, Michigan 48106

Dr. David Summers, Battelle Human Affairs Research Center, 4000 N.E. 41st Street, Seattle, Washington 98105

Professor Lester Thurow, Department of Economics, Massachusetts Institute of Technology, Cambridge, Massachusetts 02137

Professor Walter Weisskopf, Professor of Economics Emeritus, Roosevelt University, Chicago. Current address: 675 Sharon Park Drive, 319 Menlo Park, California 94025

Dr. Kenneth Wigley, Battelle Seattle Research Center, 4000 N.E. 41st Street, Seattle, Washington 98105

AUTHOR INDEX

SUBJECT INDEX